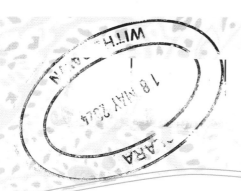
SEW
what you
LOVE

SEW
what you
LOVE

THE EASIEST, PRETTIEST PROJECTS EVER

TANYA WHELAN

POTTER CRAFT

NEW YORK

Copyright © 2011 by Tanya Wendelken

All rights reserved.

Published in the United States by Potter Craft,
an imprint of the Crown Publishing Group,
a division of Random House, Inc., New York.
www.crownpublishing.com
www.pottercraft.com

POTTER CRAFT and colophon is a registered trademark of Random House, Inc.

Library of Congress Cataloging-in-Publication Data
Whelan, Tanya.
  Sew what you love : the easiest, prettiest projects
ever / Tanya Whelan. — 1st ed.
      p. cm.
  ISBN-13: 978-0-307-58673-5 (alk. paper)
  ISBN-10: 0-307-58673-1 (alk. paper)
  1. Sewing. 2. Fancy work. I. Title.

TT705.W484 2011
646.2—dc22   2011003674

Cover and interior design by La Tricia Watford

Cover photographs by Tanya Whelan

Interior photographs by Tanya Whelan, Matthew
Mead, Yvonne Eijkenduijn, and Heather Weston

Styling by Tanya Whelan, Yvonne Eijkenduijn

Illustrations by Linda Whelan, Barry Becker

Technical editing by Linda Whelan

10 9 8 7 6 5 4 3 2 1

First Edition

Printed in China

For Kurt,

my life began the day I met you. You are the beginning and end of me. Every good thing in my life begins with you. Thank you for believing in me. I love you.

. . . .

For Linda Whelan,

my mother and partner in the writing of this book. You will never know how grateful I am to you for your love and support in this and all my endeavors. I couldn't have done it without you. And you'll never know, because it's impossible to express, just how much I love you.

CONTENTS

INTRODUCTION

It's not at all an exaggeration to say that sewing has been one of the most important things in my life. It's allowed me to both express my own personal creativity and make very useful, practical things. Eventually, my passion for sewing led to my career as a fabric, pattern, and housewares designer.

Many of my first sewing projects as an adult began out of necessity and frugality, including the giant pillows I made from inexpensive muslin in order to transform my studio bed into a sofa. Then there were the customized shades for the house with oddly sized windows and the sweet dress I made from dollar-a-yard calico for my baby girl. But I quickly came to appreciate the immense satisfaction that came from using things I had made myself. Sewing gave me a special kind of confidence that I could create something, that I could make an attractive—and functional—item from a flat piece of cloth.

Each project in this book expresses my love of sewing simple, pretty, and useful things: Bags because you can't have enough, and they're just so darn useful and therefore incredibly gratifying to make. Projects for kids because sewing for children is fun. Making things for kids inspires new possibilities that you wouldn't necessarily pursue when sewing for yourself. Home projects because it's lovely to put your own individual stamp on your home with handmade items. And easily achievable, modern adult clothing, items that people often are, unnecessarily, nervous about attempting for themselves.

All the projects are simple and can be made by even novice sewers. And for experienced sewers, these projects and patterns are guaranteed to work well and produce a beautiful end result.

In addition to the projects, this book offers simple techniques meant to be built upon. Learning a great way to make a fabric box, a patchwork ball, or an integrated handle for a bag opens up a world of creative possibilities that I hope you'll explore and use to create your own designs.

HOW TO USE THIS BOOK

This book contains almost thirty projects, plus directions for a few more quick projects, which are easy to sew, no matter your skill level. While I don't go into sewing basics, the information contained in the beginning section of the book will help get you started making these designs. I include some of my tried-and-true sewing principles, give you a brief glossary of sewing terms, explain the basic tools and materials you should have on hand, and provide a basic guide for choosing and using the fabrics recommended for the projects in this book. Most, if not all, of the projects in this book require a sewing machine, thread, pins, scissors, a ruler or yardstick, a pencil, and perhaps a hand-sewing needle once in a while. Rather than repeat this list for each project, since these items are probably already in your sewing box, I simply identify them in the directions as *Your Sewing Box*. Anything else you need will be listed under *Supplies* in the directions for each project.

The book's projects are divided into bags, home projects, children's projects, and personal style. All of the projects are very approachable even for beginner sewers. Even if you've never sewn before, you should give these pieces a try. My only advice to those who have literally never stitched a seam is to read your sewing machine's manual to

get familiar with the basics of how to use it. Honestly, the most difficult part of sewing is often just getting used to the inevitable mishaps that happen while using even the best sewing machines. A needle breaking or a bobbin getting tangled is simply par for the course, but the more familiar you are with how your machine works the better you'll be able to manage these things when they happen. Before jumping into the projects here, just practice. Sew some pillows, practice sewing around curves and corners, practice sewing through layers of interfacing and fabric, try different stitches, stitch lengths and tensions to understand how they work. In other words, just get enough practice on your machine so that you feel really comfortable using it, and then you're ready to try the projects in this book.

These projects were designed to be fairly simple to make, without a lot of difficult detailing, but with great shape and modern yet classic—and yes, pretty—style that will be enhanced with your choice of fabric.

Patterns for the projects that call for them can be found in the envelope at the back of the book. See page 17 for information on how to use the patterns and templates.

Seam allowances throughout the book are $\frac{1}{4}$" (6mm) unless otherwise noted.

GENERALLY GOOD SEWING PRINCIPLES

While the projects in this book don't necessarily require meticulous precision, there are some good sewing practices that both the easygoing as well as the perfectionist sewer should keep in mind.

✤ Prepare your fabrics

Always wash, dry, and press your washable fabrics before beginning a project. If you don't, your finished creation may shrink the first time you launder it. This step is a little bit of a hassle but well worth it.

✤ Press things

If you keep your iron handy, you won't be sorry. Pressing fabrics makes them easier to work with. Check your iron settings when pressing fabric and never place a hot iron directly on top of interfacing, as it may melt. When in doubt, iron a delicate piece using a layer of scrap fabric.

✤ Lock your seams

Remember to make a backstitch or two at the start and end of every seam. If you don't, your seam can pull apart at the edges.

✤ Pin the right way

In most cases, it's best to insert your pins perpendicular to the seam you'll be sewing. This makes it much easier to pull them out as you sew.

✤ It's okay if you hate to baste

Basting (adding long temporary stitches by hand or sewing machine) interfacing to fabric keeps the two pieces together as you work. But many sewers won't baste even if you pay them. Pinning is the next best thing, and in a pinch, even ironing the fabrics together can be helpful.

✤ Play around

Don't be afraid to experiment. Sew smaller pieces of fabric together to custom-make your own material. Introduce hand embroidery or quilting to your fabric, bring in fancy buttons, or repurpose an old, pretty tablecloth, sheet, or shirt—unique details like these can add soul and personality to your projects and give you the opportunity to try new techniques.

✤ Read first, sew second

I used to hate reading directions, preferring to dive right into sewing. But if you invest a few short minutes reading through the instructions, you will better understand the flow of things and won't be surprised or confused along the way.

◀ **There are no hard rules about fabric**

Fabric can be light, medium, or heavy in weight, as well as stiff or soft in feel. Interfacing can be regular woven fabric, fleece, a stabilizer like Pellon, or other things. The combination of fabric and interfacing gives an item its heft. If you want to use canvas for the outside of a handbag, you might want a medium-weight lining and light-weight interfacing, or no interfacing at all. I've suggested combinations that I know work, but there are others. If you need help, consult your fabric supplier.

◀ **Don't be too fussy**

Nobody will see that tiny bump at the bottom of your bag, which happened when the dog stepped on your foot pedal. Some things are not worth fixing.

◀ **Reuse, repurpose, and refashion**

Before you discard jeans, tops, and handbags, save the zippers, buttons, and hardware. These can generally be reused and will come in handy for your sewing projects as well as for minor repairs. You can use old pillows for stuffing and cut up old comforters for baby blankets. The felt from really inexpensive little blankets can be used for appliqués and flowers. Try to refashion pieces: Extend the use of kids' jeans another season by cutting them right below the zipper and sewing a long ruffle to the edge for a skirt.

◀ **The best sewing advice my mother ever gave me**

If you get angry, put it down and come back later.

SEWING TERMS USED IN THIS BOOK

None of the projects in this book require superfancy techniques that need a lot of explanation. That said, here are some brief descriptions of terms I've used throughout the book.

Baste. Hand- or machine-sewing a long, straight stitch. Use this to temporarily hold layers of fabric (or fabric and interfacing) together. If it shows, you can cut and pull out basting stitches after they've served their purpose.

Clip curves. Making a small cut on the seam allowance perpendicular to the seam helps to produce a nice smooth curve when the item is turned right side out. Be careful not to snip through the seam allowance.

Cutting on the fold. This is when you fold the fabric, place the pattern piece on the folded edge, and cut it out to create a full piece. Think about tracing the edge of half a heart on the folded edge of a piece of paper. When you cut it out you end up with a full heart.

Dart. Darts are small sewn tucks used to shape fabric and are often used to make fabric conform to a body.

Gather. A gather is made by stitching along one edge of a piece of fabric and then gently pulling one of the threads so that the fabric bunches up along the length of the thread. It's a good idea to sew two lines of stitching close together when gathering so that if one thread breaks while gathering you can continue the gather using the other stitch line.

Hook-and-loop tape. You probably know what this is already, but for anyone who doesn't, it's more often referred to by the trademark name Velcro. The "hook" side is the rough side; the "loop" side is the soft side.

Interfacing. A material, usually synthetic, used underneath fabric to give the finished project more weight, body or stiffness. It comes in many different weights from very thin to thick and stiff. Interfacing comes in both "sewn in" or fusible (an iron is used to fuse the interfacing to the fabric) types.

Pleat. Pleats are made by folding fabric over on itself, pressing, and then stitching in place. This creates volume in the fabric that falls below the stitched portion of a pleat.

Raw edges. The cut, unsewn edge of the fabric.

Right side. The printed or front side of the fabric.

Seam allowance. Seam allowance is the distance between the stitch line and the edge of the fabric. Most of the projects in this book use a $\frac{1}{4}$" (6mm) seam allowance which allows you to line up the side of the presser foot of your sewing machine to the edge of the fabric and use the side of the presser foot as your guide.

Sew or stitch. Stitching two pieces of fabric together to form a seam.

Stitch in the ditch. This is a common quilting term meaning to stitch very close to—but not quite on top of—a seam on the right side of the project. This is a type of topstitching.

Topstitch. A stitch that is made on top of the fabric, usually on the right side of the material. Unlike simply sewing or stitching to join two pieces of fabric which form a seam, topstitching will usually be visible on the outside of the project and is often used as a decorative finishing detail. On a typical buttoned down shirt, for example, the stitching that joins the front and back of the shirt will not be visible when the shirt is right side out, but the collar, cuffs, and button placket will all have visible topstitching.

Trim corners. Trimming corners means snipping off the corner to reduce the bulk so that when the item is turned right side out, the corner will be sharp. Be very careful not to cut the corner itself—you just want to clip to within $\frac{1}{16}$" (1mm) of the corner stitching.

Whipstitch. A simple hand stitch that can be used to close an open portion of a seam that can't be neatly finished with the machine. For example, if a pillow cover is turned right side out and stuffed, a whipstitch can be used to close the opening. To make a whipstitch, sew through the bottom layer of fabric close to the edge, up through the top layer, and then bring the needle and thread around the edges and back through the bottom layer (as in the diagram below). The closer this stitch is done to the edge, the less noticeable it will be.

Wrong side. The unprinted or back of the fabric.

BASIC TOOLS AND MATERIALS

YOUR SEWING BOX

Most projects in this book call for some basic sewing items that every crafter should have on hand. Instead of repeating the list again and again, I've grouped them into what I'm calling *Your Sewing Box*. So whenever you see Your Sewing Box, you'll know you need these items listed below. In fact, put them in your sewing box now if they're not already there. These are really the absolute minimum tools you need for sewing anything. Anything additional is listed separately in each project under *Supplies*.

- All-purpose polyester thread that matches your fabric
- Assorted hand-sewing needles
- Large safety pins
- Sharp scissors reserved for cutting only fabric
- Small, pointy scissors for snipping threads
- Straight pins and a pincushion
- Tape measure
- Yardstick or ruler
- Iron
- Pencil with eraser

PATTERNS

Patterns, when called for, are enclosed in the envelope attached to the book. When a pattern is not overlapped with another, it can just be cut out and used by pinning it to the fabric, according to the project instructions, and cutting around it. When a pattern is overlapped with another, or if you want to keep the original pattern sheets uncut, use large sheets of tracing paper (tape the tracing paper together if necessary), lay it over the original pattern sheet and trace the pattern using a pencil, and then cut out your pattern piece. Or use a clear shower curtain and a thin permanent marker to trace the patterns. This has the advantage of being sturdier and longer lasting than tracing paper. Once the pattern is cut out, pin it to the fabric according to the layout guide for that project and cut around the pattern.

Some of the projects ask you to "transfer marks" from the pattern to the fabric. Once you've used the pattern to cut out your fabric, you then need to place the pattern on top and, using a pencil, copy the pattern markings onto the fabric by lifting the pattern and approximating the markings as accurately as you can. Where the project says to transfer "dots," you can simply poke through the paper pattern or tracing paper with your pencil where the dots are and make a mark onto the fabric.

TEMPLATES

A few of the projects in this book use templates. Photocopy or simply use a sheet of paper to trace the template before cutting it out and pinning to your fabric.

UNDERSTANDING AND USING FABRICS

Most of the projects in this book, except the knit projects, use cotton quilting fabric that is between 44" and 45" wide because it's affordable, washable, easy to work with, and readily available. This is light-weight woven, as opposed to knitted, cotton fabric. There has been a design revolution in the fabric industry over the past few years, and fabrics that in the past were used only for quilting are now being used for clothing, bags, curtains, slipcovers, and much more. Long gone are the days when quilting fabric meant tiny patterns and muted colors. Large-scaled patterns, vibrant color, and a huge variety of designs ranging from "new vintage" to very modern and contemporary are now available from local fabric stores and thousands of online retailers.

Short of using the type of fabric the project calls for, there really are no rules when it comes to choosing fabrics. Choosing fabrics that appeal to you is the fun part of sewing and where you can really express your own unique aesthetic. What you like should be your primary guide when deciding on fabrics for a particular project. That said, there are a couple of things that I keep in mind when choosing fabrics.

woven fabrics: Choose quality, 100 percent cotton, quilting fabric. Most quilting fabric, sold through independent quilting stores, have a thread count of at least 60 by 60 or 68 by 68. This just means the number of threads per square inch woven vertically and horizontally to create the fabric. Lower quality fabrics that you might find from a discount store can be tempting, as they are less expensive, but have lower thread counts and are often not 100 percent cotton. They're thinner, tend to pill more, and have less strength and durability.

Pay attention to whether the design of the fabric has a direction and make sure you cut out your pattern appropriately. For example, if you're using fabric where all the flowers are printed in one direction as opposed to scattered and you are making a skirt, you'll want to make sure that fabric pieces match and the flowers end up with the bloom on top and stem on the bottom.

In general, it is nice to use fabrics with small-scale designs for small projects and larger-scaled designs for larger projects. If you use a large-scaled design for a pincushion, for example, you won't be able to see much of the actual design. Larger projects like bags or home decor items can make more of an impact when large-scaled motifs are used.

When deciding what designs and colors to use for a project that is pieced, meaning to sew small pieces of fabric together to form a larger piece of fabric, it is obviously completely personal and subjective. However, I've found that a cohesive look can usually be achieved by choosing three to five fabrics of different scales and color that all share at least one dominant color, or to use fabrics with different colors but with similar hues or shades.

knits: Knits come in various weights, widths and with different amounts of stretch. There's a primer on sewing with knits on page 136, but when purchasing knits I look for single knit cottons with two-way (also known as four-way) stretch. Knits can be a bit trickier to work with, but I find cotton knits to be fairly easy to sew with and, unlike some synthetic knits or blends, cotton knits are washable.

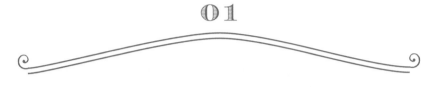

01

HANDMADE HANDBAGS

The sheer utility of handbags makes them one of my favorite things to sew. There is always a need for a bag whether for carrying groceries, beach gear, baby supplies, or just a lipstick and cell phone. Bags are also wonderful to make because they provide immediate gratification: You can sew one and use it on the same day. This chapter covers bags for every occasion. The small and feminine Amelie Bag has a sweet shape and can also be made in a larger version. The Big Easy Sling Bag is superroomy, superpractical, and seriously easy. The City Tote isn't too big nor too small, and features an easy way to achieve an integrated handle. The Zoe Bag has a structured, old fashioned feel. And the Pretty Pleated Clutch is perfect for special occasions.

Each of these projects tackles some of the different aspects of bag construction, including using darts to create volume, making a seamless, integrated handle, or using new materials like heavy-weight interfacing to make shapes that in the past required a metal frame. Once you become familiar with some of these techniques, I hope you'll use them to create your own designs.

AMELIE BAG

This bag is pretty, practical, and feminine. Make the larger version for days when you need to carry it all, and use the smaller size when all you need is a lipstick, your wallet, and maybe your iPod. Use a ¼" (6mm) seam allowance unless the directions specify otherwise.

STEP 1. *cut out the pieces.*

Using the Amelie Bag pattern and following the diagram, cut out the following:

From fabric A, cut two bags and two 2" x 15½" (5cm x 38cm) straps.

From fabric B (lining fabric), cut two bags and two 2" x 15½" (5cm x 38cm) straps.

From leftover fabric B, cut one 8" x 10" (20.5cm x 25.5cm) pocket piece (not shown).

From interfacing, cut two bags and two 2" x 15½" (5cm x 38cm) straps.

FINISHED MEASUREMENTS

Larger bag: 38" wide x 24" tall (96.5cm x 61cm)

Smaller bag: 38" wide x 19" tall (96.5cm x 48.5cm)

YARDAGE

⅝ yd (57cm) for the larger bag or ½ yd (45.5cm) for the smaller bag of 44/45" (112/114cm) cotton print for bag and straps (fabric A)

⅞ yd (80cm) for the larger bag or ¾ yd (68.5cm) for the smaller bag of 44/45" (112/114cm) cotton solid or print for lining and pocket (fabric B)

1¼ yd (1.1m) of 20" (51cm) medium-weight sew-in interfacing

SUPPLIES

• Amelie Bag pattern

• Your Sewing Box

• Magnetic snap

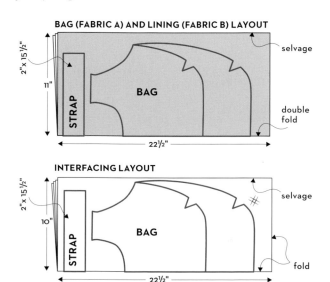

STEP 2. *interface the bag pieces.*

Transfer the dots for the pleats from the pattern to the right side of the fabric A bag pieces with a pencil mark. Pin (or hand-baste) the interfacing to the wrong side of the fabric A bag pieces. Trim ½" (13mm) from the ends of each strap interfacing. Pin (or hand-baste) the interfacing to the wrong side of the fabric A straps, centering it between the ends.

STEP 3. *sew the darts.*

With the right sides together, sew the darts on the interfaced bag and lining pieces.

STEP 4. *add the pocket and snap.*

With right sides together, fold the pocket piece in half so that it's 8" wide x 5" long (20.5cm x 12.5cm). Sew the raw edges together, leaving a 2" (5cm) opening. Trim the corners. Turn right side out and press flat.

Center and pin the pocket to the right side of one fabric B lining piece 1" (2.5cm) from bottom, and then topstitch along the seamed edges. Topstitch a vertical line 3" (7.5cm) from the left side of the pocket to form two compartments. Install a magnetic snap 1" (2.5cm) from the top edge of the lining, following the manufacturer's instructions. Use a small piece of interfacing behind the snap to reinforce the fabric.

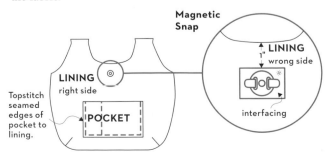

STEP 5. *sew the bag and lining.*

With right sides facing, sew the fabric A bag pieces together along the sides and bottom edges. Repeat with the fabric B lining pieces but leave a 4" (10cm) opening in the bottom seam.

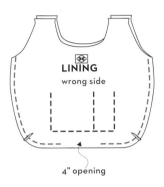

STEP 6. *join the bag and lining.*

Place the bag inside the lining with right sides facing and pin together. Sew the lining to the bag along the top edges of the front, back, and sides, leaving the strap ends open. At the strap openings, trim the interfacing close to the stitching to reduce bulk. Turn the bag right side out gently through the opening in the lining bottom. Fold and press the raw edges of the opening under, and topstitch close to the edge. Arrange the pieces so that you have a bag with the lining inside. Press the top edges.

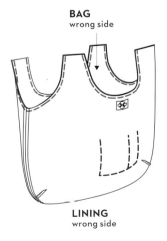

STEP 7. *make the pleats.*

Make pleats at each strap end (see pattern and diagram). The pleated end should measure 1½" (3.8cm) across when you're done, so adjust the pleat accordingly. Press the pleats away from the center and pin. Sew along the top edge to anchor each pleat.

Stitch along edge to anchor pleats.

1½"

STEP 9. *stitch the straps closed.*

Tuck the pleated end inside one strap and tuck the lining under by ½" (13mm). Press neatly. Topstitch very close to the seam, or whipstitch it closed. Repeat with the remaining strap, as shown.

Insert bag into opening in strap. Tuck linning under. Hand stitch closed or stitch in the ditch, being sure to catch the lining in your stitching.

BAG
right side

STEP 8. *make and add the straps.*

With right sides together, sew the long edges of the interfaced fabric A strap and strap lining together, leaving the first and last ½" (13mm) unsewn. Trim the interfacing close to the seam. Turn the strap right side out using a safety pin. If you've never done this before, pin a safety pin to the opening at one end, and then insert the head of the pin into the same opening it's pinned to. Gather the fabric along the pin and pull it backward until the pin comes out the other side and the strap is turned right side out. Press flat. Repeat to make a second strap. With right sides together, sew the fabric A side of the strap to the pleated strap end on the fabric A side of the bag using a ½" (13mm) seam.

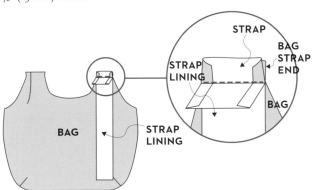

STRAP

BAG STRAP END

STRAP LINING

BAG

BAG

STRAP LINING

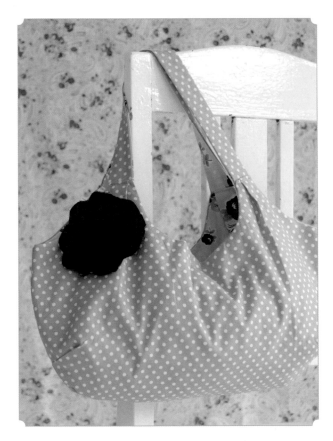

THE BIG EASY SLING BAG

Well, it's quite big, it's easy to make, and it sort of looks like a sling, hence the name. This is a big unstructured bag that will look stylish even when you are carrying a lot of stuff around. It is ideal for shopping trips or for toting to the gym. Use a ¼" (6mm) seam allowance unless the directions specify otherwise.

FINISHED MEASUREMENTS
20" wide x 33" tall (51cm x 84cm)

YARDAGE
1 yd (91cm) 44/45" (112/114cm) cotton print for bag exterior (fabric A)

1 yd (91cm) 44/45" (112/114cm) cotton solid or print for lining and pocket (fabric B)

SUPPLIES
• Big Easy Sling Bag pattern

• Your Sewing Box

• One button

STEP 1. *cut out the pieces.*

Using the Big Easy Sling Bag pattern and following the diagram, cut out the following:

From fabric A, cut two bags.

From fabric B, cut two bags and one 10" x 12" (25.5cm x 30.5cm) pocket piece.

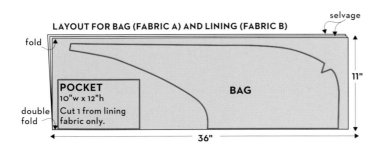

STEP 2. *sew the darts.*

With right sides together, sew the darts on the bag (fabric A) and the lining (fabric B) pieces.

BAG
wrong side

STEP 3. *make and add the loop closure.*

From leftover fabric A, cut a 1" x 4½" (2.5cm x 11.5cm) strip on the bias. Fold it in half lengthwise and press flat. Fold the long raw edges under again by ¼" (6mm), and press all layers together. Topstitch close to the edge. Fold in half to form a loop. Center the raw ends of the loop on the right side of the fabric A bag at the top center, and anchor with a few stitches along the edge.

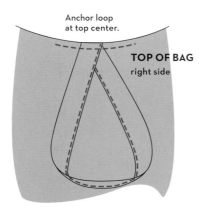

Anchor loop
at top center.

TOP OF BAG
right side

STEP 4. *sew the bag.*

With right sides together, pin and sew the fabric A bag pieces along the edge from the top of one strap, along the bottom of the bag, and up the other strap. Press the side seams open at the top.

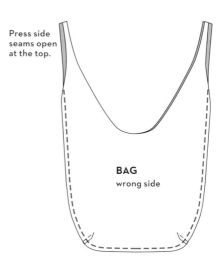

Press side
seams open
at the top.

BAG
wrong side

STEP 5. *add the pocket.*

With right sides together, fold the pocket piece in half so that it's 10" wide x 6" tall (25.5cm x 15cm). Sew the raw edges together, leaving a 2" (5cm) opening. Trim the corners. Turn right side out, and poke out the corners with the eraser end of a pencil. Center and pin the pocket to the lining 3" (7.5cm) from the bottom. Topstitch the pocket to the lining along the seamed edges. Topstitch a vertical line down the middle (or where desired) to make two compartments.

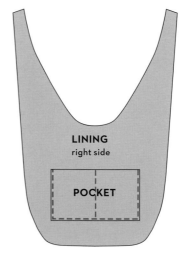

LINING
right side

POCKET

STEP 6. *make the lining bag.*

With right sides together, pin and sew the lining pieces (fabric B) along the outer edge from the top of the strap, along the bottom, and up the other strap, but leave a 4" (10cm) opening in the bottom.

STEP 7. *join the bag and lining.*

Place the lining inside the bag with right sides together. Pin the top edges together and sew the lining to the bag all around the top edges and straps. Trim corners at the top to reduce bulk. Turn the bag right side out through the opening in the lining bottom, and arrange the pieces so that you have a bag with the lining inside. Use the eraser end of a pencil to gently poke out the straps. Tuck the raw edges of the lining opening under by $\frac{1}{4}$" (6mm), and topstitch close to the edge.

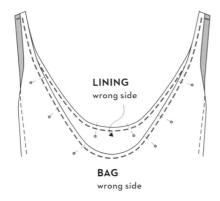

LINING
wrong side

BAG
wrong side

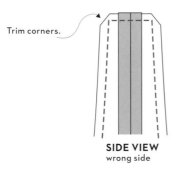

Trim corners.

SIDE VIEW
wrong side

STEP 8. *add the button.*

Attach a button at the top center of the bag, aligned properly with the loop. Press the top edges and strap. Tie the ends together.

ZOE BAG

I love the structured bags from the '50s that used a hard frame or were made completely from melamine or Lucite. Think Mad Men with all those tailored, fitted dresses, and matching purses. This bag uses extrastiff, heavy-weight interfacing to achieve a similar result. Depending on the fabric, it's perfect for special occasions or the office, but it can also work great as a contrast to jeans and a casual top. Use a ¼ " (6mm) seam allowance unless the directions specify otherwise.

FINISHED MEASUREMENTS
16" wide x 6 ½ " tall (40.5cm x 16.5cm)

YARDAGE
¾ yd (68.5cm) of 44/45" (112/114cm) cotton print for bag exterior (fabric A)

⅜ yd (34.5cm) of 44/45" (112/114cm) cotton solid or print for lining (fabric B)

⅝ yd (57cm) of 20" (51cm) heavy-weight sew-in interfacing (such as Pellon 70)

SUPPLIES
• Zoe Bag pattern

• Your Sewing Box

• 2" (5cm) piece of ½" (13mm) sew-on hook-and-loop tape

STEP 1. *cut out the pieces.*

Using the Zoe Bag pattern and following the diagram, cut out the following:

From fabric A, cut two 13½" x 18" (34.5cm x 45.5cm) rectangles for the bag, one 3" x 21" (7.5cm x 53.5cm) strap, and one 5" x 27" (12.5cm x 68.5cm) tab closure.

From fabric B, cut two bags.

From the interfacing, cut two bags (noting the cutting line on the pattern) and one 1⅛" x 20" (2.8cm x 51cm) strap.

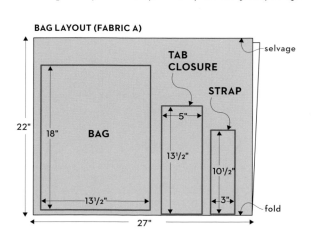

BAG LAYOUT (FABRIC A)

LINING LAYOUT (FABRIC B)

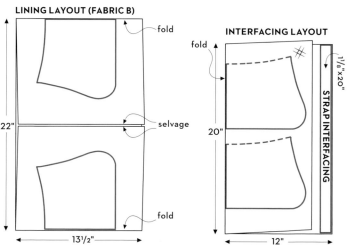

INTERFACING LAYOUT

STEP 2. *trace the top of bag onto fabric.*

Place both fabric A rectangles on a flat surface with wrong sides together. Center the bag interfacing on the top edge of the rectangle. Trace the top curve of the bag shape onto the fabric. Cut along this line. Do not cut the entire bag pattern out of the fabric.

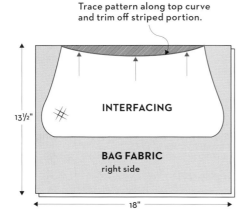

Trace pattern along top curve and trim off striped portion.

13½"

INTERFACING

BAG FABRIC
right side

18"

STEP 3. *make the front and back of the bag.*

Fold fabric A rectangle in half and press to mark a center line. Without locking stitches (or backstitching), stitch along the crease using a long basting stitch. Pull one thread to gather the fabric. Mark the center of the interfacing with a vertical pencil line. Pin the interfacing to the wrong side of the fabric, aligning the gathered seam with the drawn center line on the interfacing. Extend the fabric past the top and bottom of the interfacing by ½" (13mm). Topstitch the fabric to the interfacing vertically along the gathering line. Arrange the gathers in a way that pleases you—the fabric should stretch nicely across the interfacing so that it isn't at all baggy. Use lots of pins in the middle (not on the edges), or press to flatten out the gathers.

STEP 4. *join the bags together.*

On both pieces, fold the excess fabric over the top of the interfacing and press flat. Pin and baste the interfacing ⅛" (3mm) from the edge, encasing the top of the interfacing. Repeat on the bottom edge of the interfacing. With right sides together, pin and sew the bottom of the interfacing pieces together, sewing only the straight portion of the bottom, not up the curved corner or sides.

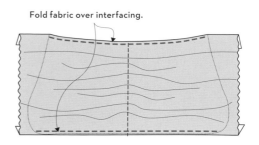

Fold fabric over interfacing.

STEP 5. *topstitch the tab closure.*

Press the long edges of the tab under by 1¼" (3cm), creating a tab 2½" (6.5cm) wide. Lay the bag flat (butterfly-style) with the right side up. Center the tab over the center gathering line, and pin it to the bag, letting it hang over the top edge by 4" (10cm) and the bottom edge by 9½" (24cm). Topstitch the sides of the tab ⅛" (3mm) from the edges, making sure it's nice and flat as you sew. Make a pencil mark 3" (7.5cm) down from top of bag on the front tab strip, ending at the top of the bag. Align the bottom of the hooked tape on the mark and topstitch through both the tab and bag.

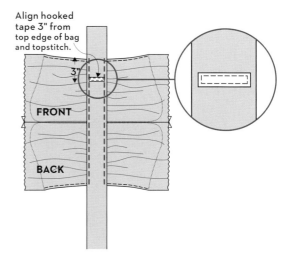

Align hooked tape 3" from top edge of bag and topstitch.

3"

FRONT

BACK

STEP 6. *join the sides of the bag.*

Fold the bag along the bottom seam so that the right sides are facing. Pin and sew both curved sides through the interfacing and fabric. Trim excess fabric flush with the interfacing. Gently turn the bag right side out.

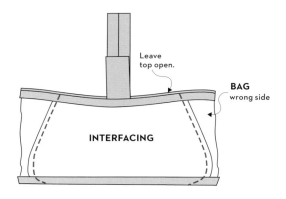

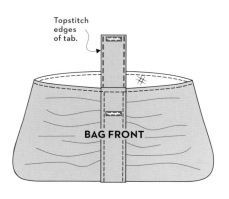

STEP 7. *finish the tab closure.*

Tuck 4" (10cm) of the front tab inside the bag and topstitch ⅛" (3mm) from the top edge. On the longer tab, measure 3½" (9cm) from the edge of the bag, fold, and press.

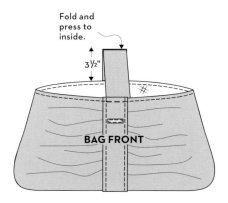

Unfold the tab and topstitch a 2" (5cm) piece of looped tape to the tab ⅛" (3mm) above the fold line, adjusting the placement as needed to make it align with the hooked tape on the front. Fold the tab inside the bag. Pin and topstitch the tab ⅛" (3mm) from each long edge down to 1" (2.5cm) past the top edge of the bag.

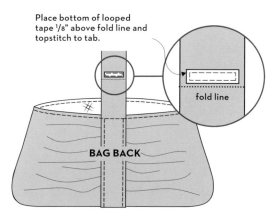

STEP 8. *make the strap.*

Fold the 21" x 3" (53.5cm x 7.5cm) strap in half lengthwise, right sides facing. Sew ¼" (6mm) from the long raw edge. Turn the strap right side out using a safety pin. If you've never done this before, pin a safety pin to the opening at one end, and then insert the head of the pin into the same opening it's pinned to. Gather the fabric along the pin and pull it backward until the pin comes out the other side and the strap is turned right side out. Attach the safety pin to the short end of the interfacing, and thread it through the strap. Making sure the strap seam and the edge of the interfacing are aligned, topstitch ⅛" (3mm) from the edge. Pin the strap inside the bag, ½" (13mm) down from the top edge, centering it on the side seams. Topstitch the strap to the inside of the bag, ⅛" (3mm) from the top edge.

STEP 9. *make the lining.*

With right sides together, pin and sew the lining pieces around the sides and bottom, leaving the top open. Press the top edge under by ½" (13mm). With wrong sides facing and aligning the side seams and top edges, pin the lining inside the bag. Topstitch ⅛" (3mm) from the top edge through all layers. Remove the basting stitches.

CITY TOTE

An integrated handle, meaning a handle that is part of the bag as opposed to being a separate strap that is sewn to the bag, makes a modern, streamlined design statement. Once you learn to make one you can build a bag design around it. The most difficult part to making one is achieving a neat professional-looking finish. The technique used for this bag achieves that. Use a ¼" (6mm) seam allowance unless the directions specify otherwise.

FINISHED MEASUREMENTS
18½" wide x 21½" tall (47cm x 55cm)

YARDAGE
¾ yd (68.5cm) of 44/45" (112/114cm) cotton print for bag exterior (fabric A)

¾ yd (68.5cm) of 44/45" (112/114cm) cotton solid or print for lining (fabric B)

1½ yd (1.4m) of 20" (51cm) medium-weight sew-in interfacing

SUPPLIES
• City Tote pattern

• Your Sewing Box

STEP 1. *cut out the bag pieces.*

Using City Tote pattern, cut out two bags from fabric A, two from fabric B, and two from the interfacing, as in the diagram. Pin or hand-baste the interfacing to the wrong side of both fabric A pieces.

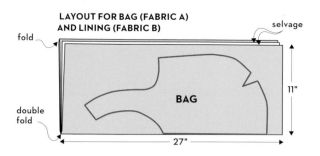

LAYOUT FOR BAG (FABRIC A) AND LINING (FABRIC B)

fold

selvage

double fold

BAG

11"

27"

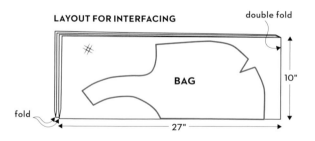

LAYOUT FOR INTERFACING

double fold

BAG

10"

fold

27"

STEP 2. *sew the darts.*

With right sides together, sew the darts on the bottom of the fabric A bag pieces using a ¼" (6mm) seam. Repeat with the fabric B lining. To add a pocket, cut a 9" x 10" (23cm x 25.5cm) rectangle from the remaining fabric B (or use a contrasting fabric), and follow step 5 of the Big Easy Sling Bag (page 28), placing the pocket at least 1" (2.5cm) above the bottom.

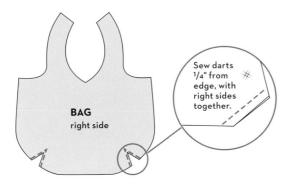

Sew darts ¼" from edge, with right sides together.

BAG
right side

STEP 3. *make the bag and lining.*

With right sides together, sew the bottom and sides of the fabric A bag pieces together along the outer edges, and turn right side out. Repeat with the lining, but leave a 5" (12.5cm) opening in the middle of the bottom. Place the bag inside the lining, with right sides facing.

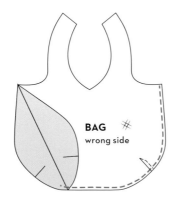

BAG
wrong side

STEP 4. *sew the lining to the bag.*

Sew the outside edges of the lining and the bag handles together. Sew the inside edges of the handles together, leaving a 5" (12.5cm) opening at both ends. Pull the bag gently through the opening in the lining bottom. Gently pull the handles right side out. Press the raw edges of the lining opening under, and topstitch ⅛" (3mm) from the edge.

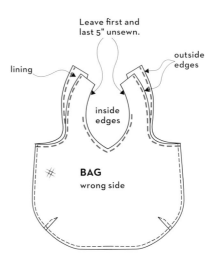

Leave first and last 5" unsewn.

lining

outside edges

inside edges

BAG
wrong side

STEP 5. *sew the handles.*

With right sides facing, sew the front handle edges together, matching the middle seams. You will have to twist the handle in order to get it under the presser foot. Press the seam open, and press the raw edges to the inside of the handle by ¼" (6mm). Repeat with the back handle.

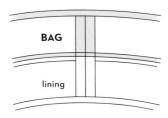

BAG

lining

With wrong sides together, fold both handles along the long seam and neatly press the edges of the bag. Topstitch ⅛" (3mm) from the top edges to finish the unsewn portion of the handle and give a nice finishing detail to the bag.

PRETTY PLEATED CLUTCH

PRETTY PLEATED CLUTCH

This clutch has classic old-fashioned appeal. It is equally wonderful when made with either a modern graphic fabric or something with a more vintage feel. For evening, try a printed or solid silk or satin. Add a Corsage Flower (page 129) for extra prettiness. The bags shown are made in cotton, perfect for a summer afternoon. Use a ¼" (6mm) seam allowance unless the directions specify otherwise.

FINISHED MEASUREMENTS
13" wide x 6¾" tall (33cm x 17cm)

YARDAGE
½ yd (45.5cm) of 44/45" (112/114cm) cotton print or solid for bag exterior (fabric A)

½ yd (45.5cm) of 44/45" (112/114cm) cotton print or solid for lining (fabric B)

½ yd (45.5cm) of 20" (51cm) heavy-weight sew-in interfacing (such as Pellon 70)

SUPPLIES
• Your Sewing Box

• 9" (23cm) of ½" (13mm) sew-on hook-and-loop tape

STEP 1. *cut out the pieces.*

Following the diagram, cut out the following:

From fabric A, cut one 23" x 13" (58.5cm x 33cm) rectangle for the bag, two 4¼" x 11" (11cm x 28cm) rectangles for the flaps, and one 2" x 30" (5cm x 76cm) strip for the trim.

From fabric B, cut one 14" x 13" (35.5cm x 33cm) rectangle for the bag lining.

From the interfacing, cut one 14" x 13" (35.5cm x 33cm) rectangle and one 1¾" x 9¼" (4.5cm x 23.5cm) strip.

LAYOUT FOR INTERFACING

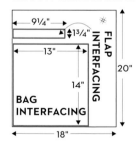

LAYOUT FOR BAG (FABRIC A)

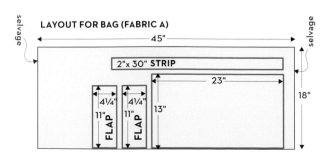

LAYOUT FOR LINING (FABRIC B)

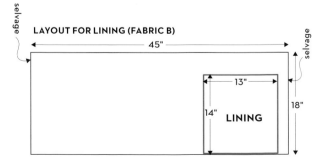

STEP 2. *make the pleats.*

On the wrong side of the fabric A rectangle, measure and mark pleats on the long edges using a ruler and pencil.

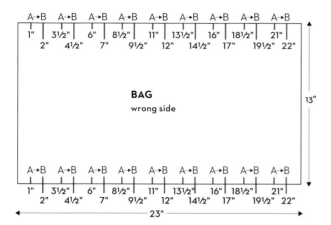

To make each pleat, pick up the fabric at point A, bring it over to point B, and pin. When all pleats are pinned, press the edges lightly to flatten the tops of the pleats. The pleated edge should be 14" (35.5cm) wide. Baste ¼" (6mm) from both edges to anchor the pleats.

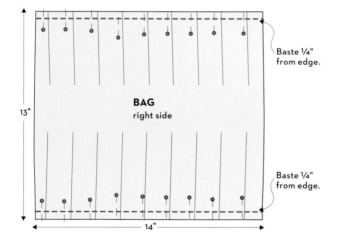

STEP 3. *sew up the sides.*

Pin and baste the interfacing to the wrong side of the bag along the 14" (35.5cm) edges. Fold the piece in half with the pleats on the inside to form a 6½" x 14" (16.5cm x 35.5cm) rectangle. (Don't let the pleats bunch up at the folded corner.) Sew the sides together through both the interfacing and fabric. Carefully trim the interfacing close to the seam. Turn right side out, and gently poke out the corners with the eraser end of a pencil.

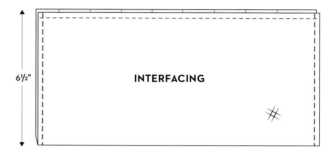

STEP 4. *line the bag.*

Fold the fabric B lining piece in half with right sides together to form a 6½" x 14" (16.5cm x 35.5cm) rectangle. Sew the short sides together. Place the lining inside the bag with the wrong side of the lining facing the interfacing. Pin the lining to the inside and sew along the top raw edge. If you have trouble maneuvering the bag because of the stiffness of the interfacing, try removing the front tray of your sewing machine (if it has one) for more ease of motion.

STEP 5. *sew on the trim strip.*

Fold one short end of the trim strip under by ½" (13mm) and press. Place the folded end of the strip at the middle of the bag and start sewing, with right sides facing, aligning the raw edges. Sew to the end of the strip, overlapping the folded edge. Fold the strip to the wrong side by ¾" (2cm), and press the crease. Fold again over the raw edge of the bag, and pin so that the trim covers the seam slightly on the inside. Carefully topstitch "in the ditch" (less than ⅛" [3mm] from the seam on trim; see page 15) on the outside of the bag making sure you are also sewing the trim on the inside of the bag as you go.

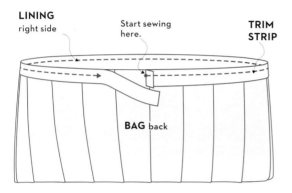

LINING
right side

Start sewing here.

TRIM STRIP

BAG back

STEP 6. *topstitch the looped strip to the flap.*

Center the looped strip of the hook-and-loop tape on the flap ½" (13mm) from the long edge and topstitch ⅛" (33mm) from the edge. With right sides facing, sew both flaps together along the long edges. Turn right side out and press.

Topstitch looped strip to flap front.

½"

FLAP right side

STEP 7. *finish the flap.*

Press both sides of the flap to the inside by ½" (13mm). Fold the flap in half lengthwise, and lightly press a crease down the middle. Topstitch along the crease. Insert the interfacing inside the top "pocket."

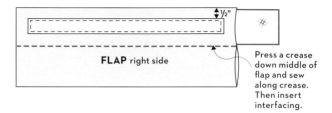

½"

FLAP right side

Press a crease down middle of flap and sew along crease. Then insert interfacing.

Topstitch ⅛" (3mm) from the edge on three sides of the flap, leaving the long edge without interfacing unstitched.

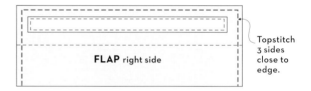

FLAP right side

Topstitch 3 sides close to edge.

STEP 8. *sew the flap to the bag.*

Align the middle line of the flap with the back of the bag (the side with binding overlap) at the top. Pin and topstitch the long edge of the flap to the bag.

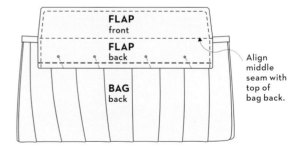

FLAP front

FLAP back

BAG back

Align middle seam with top of bag back.

STEP 9. *add the hooked strip to the bag.*

Topstitch the hooked strip of the hook-and-loop tape to the bag front, using the looped strip on the inside of the flap to guide the placement. Arrange the pleats as desired.

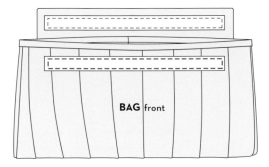

02

SEWING FOR LITTLE ONES

Sewing for children is deeply satisfying. Whether it's a blanket for a new baby, a toy, or a cute skirt that your little girl helps pick the fabric for, sewing for little ones is just another way to nurture and care for them. And when you sew for children, there are different creative possibilities you can explore by using color and pattern in fun ways that you perhaps wouldn't when sewing for yourself or your home.

This chapter provides easy-to-make projects for children of different ages, including toys, skirts, and tops. These projects feature some great basic techniques that can be built on and used in other ways. For example, the technique to make a block can also be used to make a big ottoman, a bag, or a box. The pattern for the Small Stuffed Patchwork Ball can be cut in half and, with the addition of a brim, used to make a hat. The Lila Shirred Blouse project features elastic thread which, if you've never used it before, will open up a world of creative possibilities once you get the hang of it. My favorite project in this chapter is the Made by Me! Embroidered Felt Purse, which is a simple, fun project, perfect for introducing basic sewing techniques to a child.

CONE AND STACKING LINKS

Babies will love these eye-catching soft toys, and they make a great shower gift. With the cone base, this toy is an updated version of the classic stacking rings but with a twist— the rings are open, so they double as links. This sweet toy is easy and fun to make from your fabric scraps. Use a ¼" (6mm) seam allowance unless the directions specify otherwise.

STEP 1. *cut out the cone wedges and bottom.*

Using the templates on pages 47 and 48, enlarge and cut out three Cone Wedges from the 8½" x 12" (21.5cm x 30.5cm) pieces and one Cone Bottom from the 8" x 8" (20.5cm x 20.5cm) square.

STEP 2. *join the wedges.*

With right sides facing, sew two wedges together along one straight edge, from bottom to top. Press the seam open. Add the third wedge in the same way. Sew the remaining sides together to form the cone.

FINISHED MEASUREMENTS

Cone: 10" tall 7" wide (25.5cm x 18cm)

Five links: (approximate diameter) 6½", 7½", 8½", 9½", 10½" (16.5cm, 19cm, 21.5cm, 24cm, 26.5cm)

YARDAGE

FOR THE CONE:
⅝ yd (57cm) of cotton fabric cut into three 8" x 12" (20.5cm x 30.5cm) pieces, and one 8" x 8" (20.5cm) square for the bottom

FOR THE LINKS:
¼ yd (23cm) cut into two 8" (20.5cm) square pieces for 6½" (16.5cm) link A

¼ yd (23cm) cut into two 9" (23cm) square pieces for 7½" (19cm) link B

⅜ yd (34.5cm) cut into two 10" (25.5cm) square pieces for 8½" (21.5cm) link C

⅜ yd (34.5cm) cut into two 11" (28cm) square pieces for 9½" (24cm) link D

⅜ yd (34.5cm) cut into two 12" (30.5cm) square pieces for 10½" (26.5) link E

SUPPLIES

- Cone Wedge, Cone Bottom, and Stacking Link A, B, C, D, and E templates

- Your Sewing Box

- 12-oz (340g) bag of polyester fiberfill

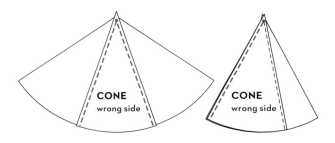

CONE
wrong side

CONE
wrong side

STEP 3. *add the bottom.*

With right sides together, pin and sew the Cone Bottom to the cone leaving a 2" (5cm) opening. Turn right side out, and stuff until you get a nice, firm, filled-out cone that can stand on its own. Use the eraser end of a pencil to get the stuffing into the pointy end. Whipstitch the opening closed.

STEP 4. *make the links.*

Using one of the Stacking Link templates, cut out two of the same-size links from contrasting fabrics. With right sides facing, pin the links together. Starting in the middle of the inner curve, sew along the edge all around, working your way back to the inner curve, leaving a 3" (7.5cm) opening and locking stitches at the beginning and end; you can use a 2" (5cm) opening on the smaller links. Clip the curves without cutting through the stitching. Turn the link right side out, and stuff with small batches of fiberfill, pushing it to the ends using the eraser end of a pencil. Fill until the link is firm and the fabric is fully stretched, and not lumpy. Whipstitch the opening closed. Make the remaining links in the same way.

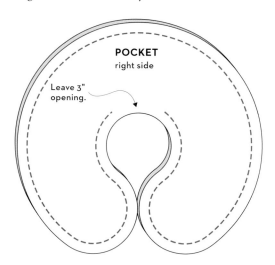

POCKET
right side

Leave 3"
opening.

CONE WEDGE TIP

Trace and connect to cone wedge bottom to make the full wedge.

CONE BOTTOM

Trace twice to make the full circle cone bottom.

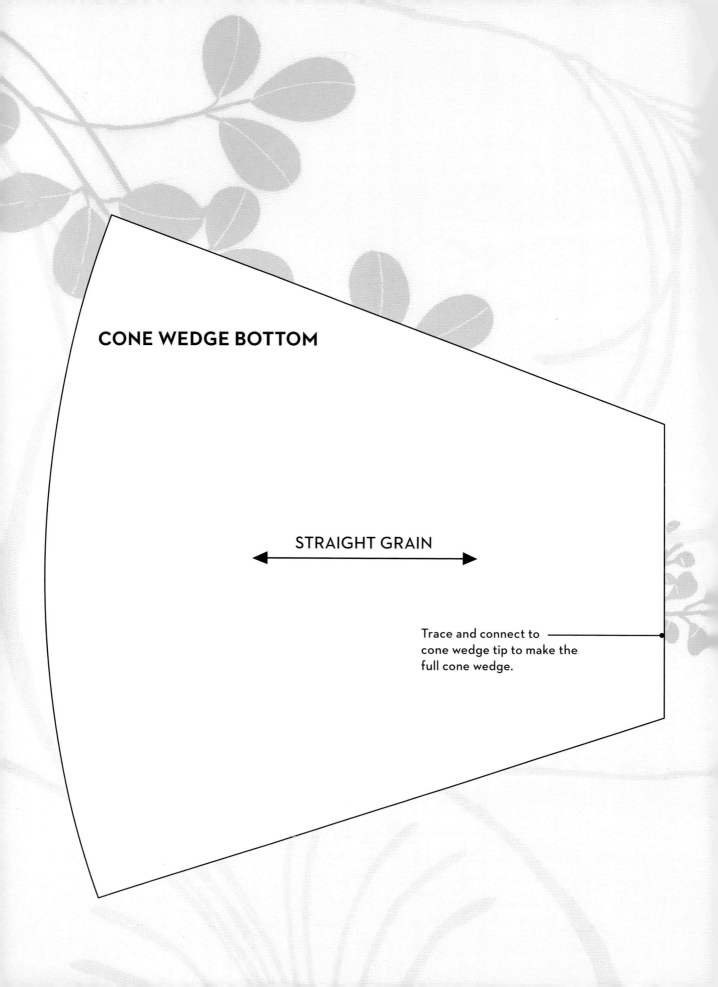

CONE WEDGE BOTTOM

STRAIGHT GRAIN

Trace and connect to
cone wedge tip to make the
full cone wedge.

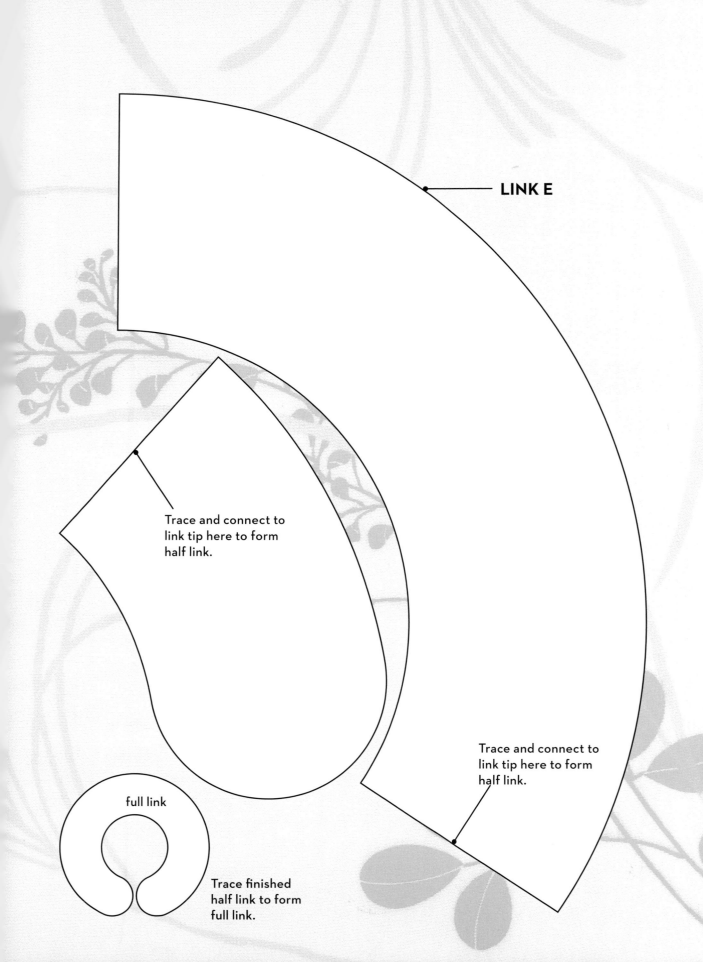

LINK E

Trace and connect to link tip here to form half link.

Trace and connect to link tip here to form half link.

full link

Trace finished half link to form full link.

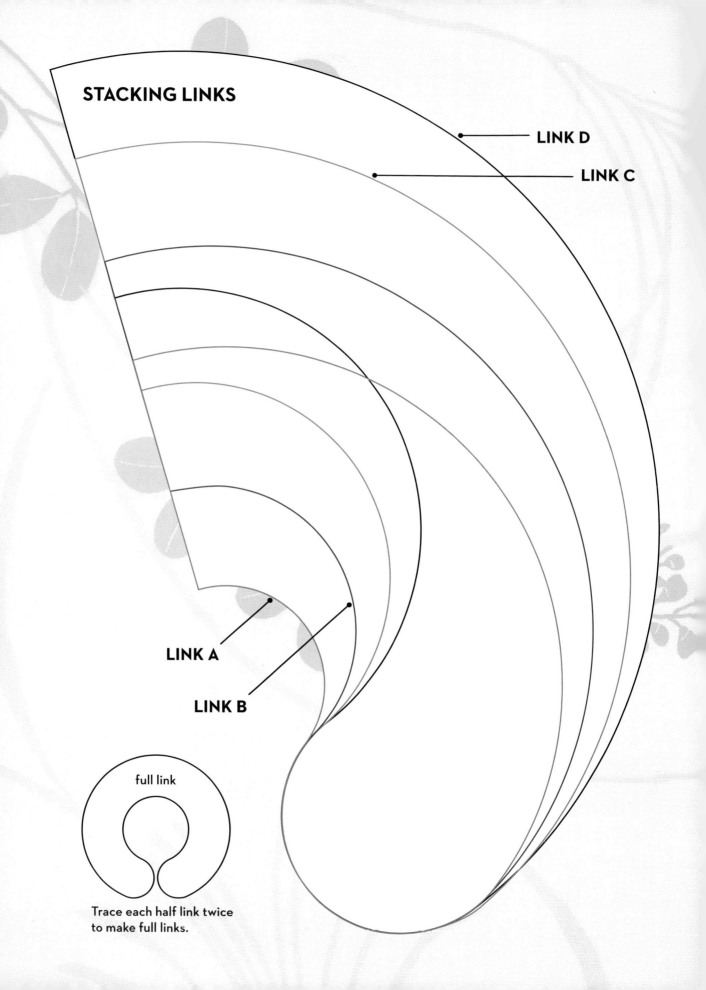

STACKING LINKS

LINK D

LINK C

LINK A

LINK B

full link

Trace each half link twice
to make full links.

MADE BY ME
EMBROIDERED
FELT PURSE

MADE BY ME! EMBROIDERED FELT PURSE

This project is a great introduction to sewing for a child and is meant to be made together with an adult. The purse is made from felt, which doesn't unravel, and it's easy to sew and embroider. It calls for freestyle embroidery and stitching in loops, zigzags, or any random pattern, and basic appliqué, emphasizing creativity and individuality rather than technique. Use a ¼" (6mm) seam allowance unless the directions specify otherwise.

FINISHED MEASUREMENTS

Bag: 8½" wide x 6½" long (21.5cm x 16.5cm)

Strap: 1" x 34" (2.5cm x 86cm), or as desired

YARDAGE

18½" x 8½" (47cm x 21.5cm) piece of wool or acrylic felt

Fabric scrap for appliqué

2½" x 36" (6.5cm x 91cm) strip of fabric for the strap

SUPPLIES

- Your Sewing Box
- Two or three colors of embroidery floss
- Embroidery needle (or any needle with an eye wide enough for the embroidery thread)
- 1" (2.5cm) button

STEP 1. *make the purse.*

Fold the felt up by 6" (15cm) and stitch ¼" from the edge down each side.

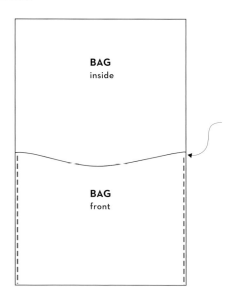

BAG
inside

BAG
front

This is where you will sew the strap (see step 4).

STEP 2. *stitch the appliqué.*

Have your child cut out a large, simple shape (such as a heart, star, circle, or square) from the fabric scrap. Pin the shape to the flap and topstitch ¹/₄" (6mm) inside the edge. Let your child stitch a freehand design on top of the shape in loops, zigzags, or whatever pleases your child.

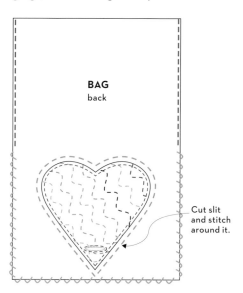

BAG
back

Cut slit and stitch around it.

STEP 3. *embroider the bag.*

Using embroidery floss, hand-embroider all around the edge of the flap using a simple whipstitch. With another color, embroider around the border of the shape and/or around the outline of the shape using a straight stitch.

STEP 4. *make the strap.*

With right sides together, fold the fabric strip in half length-wise and sew the long edges together ¹/₄" (6mm) from the edge. Using a safety pin, turn the strap right side out and press well. Tuck the short ends of the strap to the inside by ¹/₂" (13mm) and press flat. Pin and sew the strap to the underside of the flap of the purse by hand or machine.

STEP 5. *make the button closure.*

On the flap, cut a 1" (2.5cm) slit through both the fabric and felt. Stitch around the buttonhole ¹/₄" (6mm) from the edge. With the flap down against the bag front, make a little mark on the bag front (through the slit) where the button will go. Sew the button to the bag by hand using embroidery floss.

USING THE SEWING MACHINE

I can't tell you when it's safe to let a child use a sewing machine. You have to use your own best judgment as to what is safe for your child and at what age. I allow my eight-year-old daughter to sew on the machine with my supervision. I sit next to her and keep my hands close to hers to ensure she doesn't accidentally injure herself. If you don't feel comfortable letting your child use the machine, you can sew the sides and strap, and let your child sew everything else by hand. Of course, even with hand-sewing, an occasional pinprick may happen.

For practice, have your child draw shapes on felt or other fabric with a washable pencil and then stitch over the lines with different colors of thread using straight, zigzag, or fancier machine stitches.

PATCHWORK BALLS

Soft fabric balls are easy to make as well as fun and safe to play with indoors. Even my nine- and eleven-year-olds can't resist picking them up and tossing them around. The large-scale ball lets you mix eye-catching patterns, making it a great decorative item for a child's room. The smaller ones make colorful toys for babies and toddlers. They are a perfect baby shower gift, and since you can sew a bunch of them up in an afternoon, they're cute for guest favors and table decorations. Use a ¼" (6mm) seam allowance unless the directions specify otherwise.

GIANT PATCHWORK BALL

STEP 1. *cut out the pieces.*

Trace the Giant Patchwork Ball Wedge pattern and pin onto your fabrics, making sure all pieces face in the correct direction, as shown in the diagram. If you're using two fabrics to make the ball, cut out 12 wedges from fabric A and 12 from fabric B. If you're using four fabrics, cut out 6 each from fabrics A, B, C, and D.

FINISHED MEASUREMENTS
Giant patchwork ball: 58" (147cm) circumference and 18½" (47cm) diameter

Small patchwork ball: 9½" (24cm) circumference and 3" (7.5cm) diameter

YARDAGE
FOR THE GIANT PATCHWORK BALL:
¾ yd (68.5cm) each of two different cotton prints and/or solids (fabrics A and B), or ½ yd (45.5cm) each of four different prints and/or solids (fabrics A, B, C, and D)

FOR TWO SMALL PATCHWORK BALLS:
¼ yd (23cm) each of three different cotton prints and/or solids

SUPPLIES
• Giant Patchwork Ball Wedge pattern or Small Patchwork Ball pattern

• Your Sewing Box

• Two 32-oz (907g) bags of polyester fiberfill for the giant ball; one 12-oz

• (340g) bag for two small balls

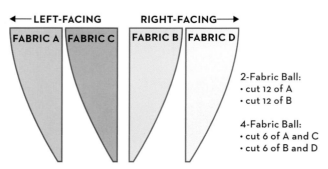

◄—LEFT-FACING   RIGHT-FACING—►

FABRIC A FABRIC C   FABRIC B FABRIC D

2-Fabric Ball:
• cut 12 of A
• cut 12 of B

4-Fabric Ball:
• cut 6 of A and C
• cut 6 of B and D

STEP 2. *arrange the pieces.*

Arrange four pieces into six groups, each group forming a wedge, to see how you want to arrange them. Move them around until you have a pattern you like.

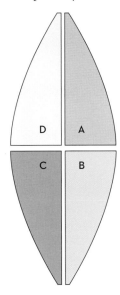

STEP 3. *form the wedges.*

With right sides facing, sew the top two quadrants of each wedge together, and then the bottom two. Press the seams open. Sew the two halves together, matching seams, and press the seams open. Make five more wedges in the same way.

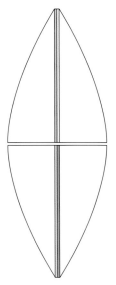

STEP 4. *assemble the ball.*

With right sides facing, sew two wedges together along a long curved edge, matching up the middle seams. Sew on a third wedge, forming one-half of the ball. Repeat with the remaining three wedges. With right sides together, sew the two halves together, leaving a 5" (12.5cm) opening along one side for turning right side out. Sew and backstitch over the top and bottom of the ball, where all the wedges meet, to ensure there is no hole there.

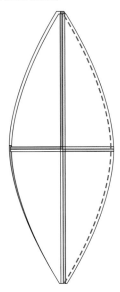

STEP 5. *stuff the ball.*

Gently turn the ball right side out, stuff with fiberfill until the fabric is stretched and the ball is firm, and whipstitch the opening closed.

SMALL PATCHWORK BALLS

STEP 1. *cut out the pieces.*

Trace and cut out two wedges from each of your three
fabrics using the Small Patchwork Ball pattern.

STEP 2. *join wedges together.*

Arrange the wedges into a pattern you like. With right sides
together, sew three wedges together to form half a ball.
Sew the three remaining wedges together. With right sides
together, sew the two halves of the ball all the way around,
leaving a 3" (7.5cm) opening along one side for turning.

STEP 3. *stuff and finish ball.*

Gently turn the ball right side out, stuff with fiberfill, and
whipstitch the opening closed.

RUFFLE-MANIA SKIRT

I've made many different versions of this skirt over the years. I love the way the ruffled layers move and twirl along with the little girl wearing it. I also love how the ruffles allow you to experiment with endless fabric combinations. After making so many skirt variations, I am confident this is the easiest, most straightforward method. You can make this skirt with one, two, or three ruffles. Remember, you can always make the strips of fabric that make up the ruffles by piecing smaller bits of fabric together. Just remember to add a ½" (13mm) seam allowance for each strip of pieced fabric. Use a ¼" (6mm) seam allowance unless the directions specify otherwise.

FINISHED MEASUREMENTS
Can be made to any size

YARDAGE
44/45" (112/114cm) cotton prints; yardage depends on child's measurements

SUPPLIES
- Your Sewing Box
- 36" (91cm) length of ½" (13mm) elastic

STEP 1. *figure the (horizontal) widths of the skirt bands and ruffles.*

Round all calculations to the nearest ¼" (6mm). Measure your child's hips at the widest part. Add 3" (7.5cm) to that measurement. This will be the final width of the skirt band or bands (the part the ruffles are sewn to). Multiply this number by 1.6. This will be the final width of each ruffle.

STEP 2. *calculate the (vertical) length of the skirt bands and ruffles.*

Round all calculations to the nearest $\frac{1}{4}$" (6mm). Measure from your child's waist (in the back) to where you want the skirt to fall; about midthigh makes a nice length for this style, but you could go longer. Divide that number by four; let's call it A.

For the one-ruffle skirt you need one band and one ruffle:
The length of the skirt band equals A + 2.25.
The length of the ruffle equals 3 x A + .75.

For the two-ruffle skirt you need two bands and two ruffles:
The length of the top skirt band equals A + 2.25.
The length of the second band equals A + .5.
The length of the top ruffle equals 2 x A.
The length of the bottom ruffle equals 2 x A + .75.

For the three-ruffle skirt you need three bands and three ruffles:
The length of the top skirt band equals A + 2.25.
The second and third bands equal A + .5.
The length of the three ruffles equals A + 1.25.

STEP 3. *cut out the pieces.*

Cut out long strips from your fabrics using the calculations you just made.

STEP 4. *make the casing for the elastic.*

Press one long edge of the top (vertically longest) band under by $\frac{3}{4}$" (2cm). Press under again by 1" (2.5cm), and topstitch close to the edge, leaving 2" (5cm) at one end unsewn. This is for inserting the elastic later.

STEP 5. *sew the ruffles.*

Without backstitching at the beginning or end, sew a basting stitch $\frac{1}{4}$" (6mm) from one long edge of each ruffle. Pull just one thread to gather the ruffle until it is the same width as the bands. Distribute the ruffles evenly along the ruffle width.

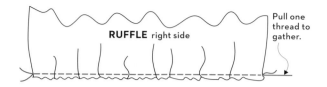

With right sides together and raw edges aligned, pin and sew one ruffle to each band. Skip to step 6 if you're making the one-ruffle skirt.

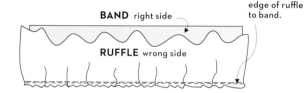

Pin and sew the right side of the second band to the underside of the seam that joins the first band and ruffle. Likewise, for the three-ruffle skirt, pin and sew the right side of the third band to the underside of the seam that joins the second band and ruffle.

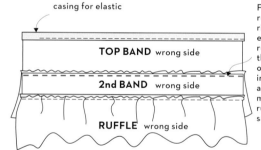

STEP 6. *sew the back seam.*

Fold the skirt in half, right sides together. For the one-ruffle skirt, with right sides together, sew the band and ruffle to form the back seam of the skirt.

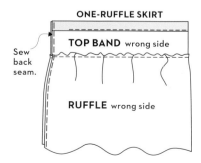

For the two- or three-ruffle skirt, with right sides together, sew the short edges of each ruffle (but not the bottom ruffle) together, being careful not to catch any other part of the skirt in the stitching.

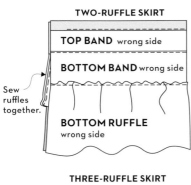

With right sides together, tuck the ruffles in and sew up the side of each band and bottom ruffle to form the back seam of the skirt. Again, be careful not to catch any other part of the skirt in the stitching. Fold and press each raw ruffle edge to the inside by $1/4$" (6mm), repeat, pin, and sew to hem.

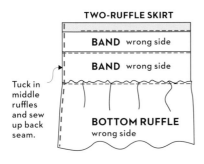

STEP 7. *add the elastic.*

Stretch the elastic around your child's waist to a length that is comfortable for her. Add about 1" (2.5cm) to this, and cut the elastic to this size. Use a safety pin to insert the elastic into the opening in the casing and pull it through. Overlap each end of the elastic by $1/2$" (13mm), and sew back and forth a few times to secure. Topstitch the opening closed.

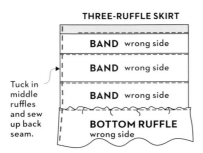

SWEET PEA BABY DUVET

This hexagon design evokes a bit of traditional American quilt flavor from the '40s, when the design was in its heyday. I used it to make a duvet (easily removable for washing) to cover a small blanket that parents can tuck into a stroller or car seat, but you can make it larger by adding hexagons. You can make a larger duvet to fit a crib comforter or make a custom blanket to fit (see step 5).

The purist's method for making a hexagon design is called "paper piecing," where you iron and/or glue fabric hexagons around individual paper templates, and then whipstitch them all together by hand. If you don't have the time for such painstaking precision, you can still achieve a perfectly charming result by machine-stitching rows of hexagons together, as I did. I used large 6" (15cm) hexagons, which made machine-piecing much easier. Use a ¼" (6mm) seam allowance unless the directions specify otherwise.

FINISHED MEASUREMENTS

Yardage and directions are given for a 23" x 26" (58.5cm x 66cm) stroller or car-seat blanket, but as a rough guideline, you can double everything for a crib-size duvet cover. Crib comforters vary a bit in size, so if you're going to purchase one, do so before you make your duvet and adapt the numbers of hexagons as needed.

YARDAGE

FOR THE DUVET:
¼ yd each of 44/45" (112/114cm) cotton prints for 30 hexagons

(¼ yd is enough for 6 hexagons)

¾ yd (68.5cm) of 44/45" (112/114cm) cotton print or solid for duvet backing

FOR THE BLANKET (optional):
¾ yd (68.5cm) of 44/45" (112/114cm) muslin and quilt batting or white fleece

SUPPLIES

- Your Sewing Box
- Hexagon pattern

STEP 1. *cut out the hexagons.*

Cut out thirty 6" (15cm) hexagons using the hexagon template (page 66). For the duvet shown, I used four coordinating fabrics. Arrange the hexagons in six rows of five, in a pattern that pleases you.

STEP 2. *sew the hexagons together.*

With right sides facing, sew the first five hexagons together, leaving $\frac{1}{4}$" (6mm) open at the beginning and end of each seam. Repeat to make six rows of joined hexagons. To make this a bit easier, you can press all sides of each hexagon under by $\frac{1}{4}$" (6mm) and make a pencil mark on the wrong sides where the folds intersect, and then sew between the dots. Press the seams open.

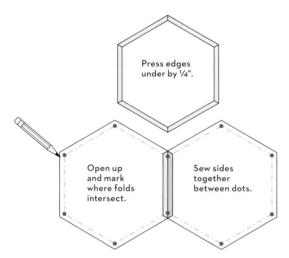

Press edges under by ¼".

Open up and mark where folds intersect.

Sew sides together between dots.

STEP 3. *sew the rows together.*

With right sides together, sew the first row to the second row, fitting the rows together as you sew and sewing between the dots. Continue sewing all the rows together. Press the duvet top well.

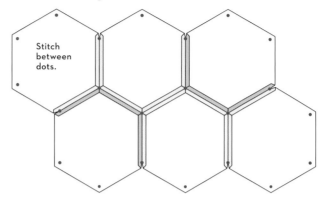

Stitch between dots.

STEP 4. *trim the duvet top.*

Cut the duvet top down to a rectangle. Measure the duvet top, and write down the length and width.

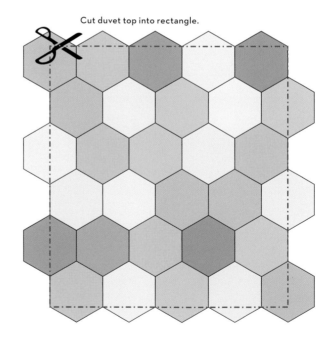

Cut duvet top into rectangle.

STEP 5. *join the duvet and backing.*

Cut two rectangles from the backing fabric. Make each rectangle the same width and three-quarters of the length of your duvet top. For example, if your duvet top is 25" (63.5cm) wide and 30" (76cm) long, cut two 25" x 22½" (63.5cm x 57cm) backing pieces. On both pieces, press the width edge (the longer edge) under by ½" (13mm), and then again by another ½" (13mm). Topstitch close to the edge. Place the duvet top right side up on a flat surface. Place the backing pieces on top, right side down, aligning the raw edges; pin and sew. Turn the duvet right side out and press well. Topstitch ¼" (6mm) from the edge along all sides.

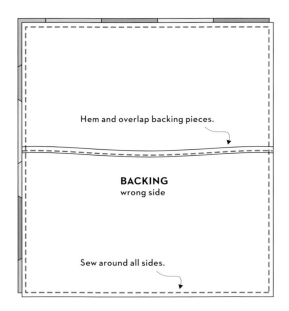

Hem and overlap backing pieces.

BACKING
wrong side

Sew around all sides.

STEP 6. *make the blanket.*

If you don't already have one, there are several easy options for making a blanket to insert inside the duvet. You can cut a piece of soft fleece ½" (13mm) smaller than your duvet—the edges don't fray, so they don't need finishing. To recycle a comforter you don't use anymore, cut off a piece to size, fold the cut edges to the inside by ½" (13mm), and topstitch.

Or make a fluffy little comforter using muslin and quilt batting. Cut two pieces of muslin and batting slightly smaller than your full duvet size. Place the batting on a flat surface. Place the two muslin pieces, with wrong sides together, on top. Pin the three layers together, and sew all around, leaving a 10" (25.5cm) opening for turning. Turn right side out, with the batting inside. Fold the edges of the opening inside, and topstitch or whipstitch close to the edge. Using a long basting stitch, topstitch three vertical and three or four horizontal evenly spaced rows through all the layers to hold the batting in place.

HEXAGON TEMPLATE

SOFT BABY BLOCKS

SOFT BABY BLOCKS

Make these sturdy fabric blocks in different sizes for tossing and playing. Coupled with a pretty fabric box or tote (page 98), they make a great gift for a toddler or a shower gift for a mother- or father-to-be. Make them in solids, too, and embellish them with embroidery or appliqué.

Using this method you can make blocks of any size, even giant cubes that make fun, squishy seating in kids' rooms. Just decide how tall and wide you want the cube to be, draw three squares of that size directly onto the wrong side of your fabric, and then follow the directions for making these baby blocks. For the giant cube pictured on this page I didn't use any interfacing, and I didn't topstitch the edges. I basically wanted just a fun giant cube pillow. You could make this sturdier by using furniture-grade foam and heavy-weight fabric. Use a ¼" (6mm) seam allowance unless the directions specify otherwise.

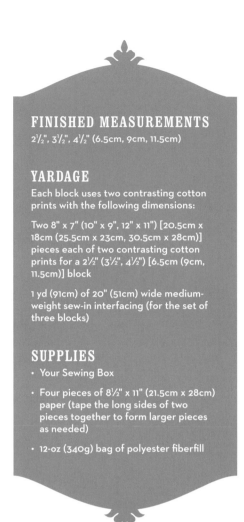

FINISHED MEASUREMENTS

2½", 3½", 4½" (6.5cm, 9cm, 11.5cm)

YARDAGE

Each block uses two contrasting cotton prints with the following dimensions:

Two 8" x 7" (10" x 9", 12" x 11") [20.5cm x 18cm (25.5cm x 23cm, 30.5cm x 28cm)] pieces each of two contrasting cotton prints for a 2½" (3½", 4½") [6.5cm (9cm, 11.5cm)] block

1 yd (91cm) of 20" (51cm) wide medium-weight sew-in interfacing (for the set of three blocks)

SUPPLIES

- Your Sewing Box

- Four pieces of 8½" x 11" (21.5cm x 28cm) paper (tape the long sides of two pieces together to form larger pieces as needed)

- 12-oz (340g) bag of polyester fiberfill

STEP 1. *make the paper patterns.*

For each block draw three squares on the paper, one on top of the other, in the dimension of the finished block (2$\frac{1}{2}$", 3$\frac{1}{2}$", and 4$\frac{1}{2}$") [6.5cm, 9cm, 11.5cm] plus $\frac{1}{2}$" (13mm) for the seam allowance. Including the seam allowance, the three squares you'll draw for each block will be 3" by 3" for the 2$\frac{1}{2}$" block, 4" by 4" for the 3$\frac{1}{2}$" block, and 5" by 5" for the 4$\frac{1}{2}$" block. Inside the top and bottom squares, draw a diagonal line from one corner to the opposite corner. Repeat with the two remaining corners, forming an X. Cut out the shape in one piece as shown in the diagram. Make patterns for the remaining blocks.

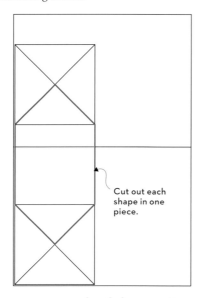

Cut out each shape in one piece.

STEP 2. *cut out the fabric and interfacing.*

For each block, pin and cut two block patterns from one fabric and two from the contrasting fabric. Cut four block patterns from the interfacing. Hand-baste the interfacing to the wrong side of each fabric piece.

STEP 3. *join the block sections.*

With the right sides of two same-size contrasting prints together, sew one side starting at the top point and ending at the bottom point. Repeat with the second pair of same-size contrasting pieces. With right sides together and alternating the prints, sew the halves together, aligning the edges and matching the seams, and leaving a 2" (5cm) opening in the middle of one side. Trim the corners slightly to reduce bulk.

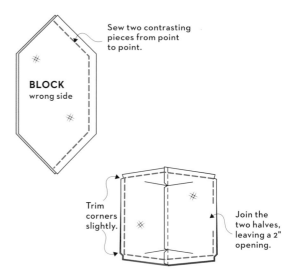

Sew two contrasting pieces from point to point.

BLOCK wrong side

Trim corners slightly.

Join the two halves, leaving a 2" opening.

STEP 4. *topstitch and stuff.*

Gently turn the block right side out and poke out the corners with a finger or the eraser end of a pencil. Press the unseamed block edges to form creases. Topstitch each crease very close to the edge, being sure to lock the stitches (page 12) at the beginning and end of each seam. Stuff the block with filling until the block is firm and the fabric is fully stretched, and not lumpy. Whipstitch the opening closed. Clip off all excess threads. Repeat steps 3 and 4 to make the other two blocks.

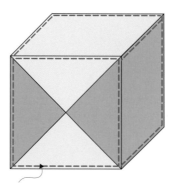

Press unseamed edges to form creases. Top-stitch each crease very close to edge.

TRAVEL CHECKERS

Finding something for kids to do on long trips is always a problem. This is a good old-fashioned solution that encourages interaction and will keep them engaged for a little while. Hopefully it will also save you from hearing "Are we there yet?" one more time. Once you arrive, use it for quiet evenings in the cabin or on picnics at the beach. The checkers are reversible, and the checkerboard serves as a storage bag. For a cute no-sew alternative, use big buttons for the checkers. It all rolls up and ties to fit neatly into your luggage.

FINISHED MEASUREMENTS
15½" x 15½" (39.5cm x 39.5cm), unrolled

YARDAGE
FOR CHECKERBOARD AND BAG:
½ yd (45.5cm) of 44/45" (112/114cm) printed cotton fabric (fabric A)

¼ yd (23cm) of 44/45" (112/114cm) contrasting printed cotton fabric (fabric B)

18" x 18" (45.5cm) square of solid-color felt for backing

FOR FELT CHECKERS:
¼ yd (23cm) each of felt in two solid (light and dark) colors

SUPPLIES
• Your Sewing Box

• Iron

• 14" (35.5cm) length of ½" (13mm) sew-in hook-and-loop tape

• 36" (91cm) length of ribbon or twill tape for tie

• Pinking shears (optional)

STEP 1. *measure and cut the fabric.*
Precision in marking and cutting will really impact the final outcome of this project. Following the diagram, measure and cut an 18" (45.5cm) square from fabric A for the bag. Then measure and cut four 2½" x 20" (6.5cm x 51cm) strips from fabric A and four from fabric B for the checkerboard.

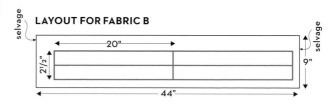

LAYOUT FOR FABRIC A

selvage · selvage · 18" · 20" · 2½" · 44" · 18"

LAYOUT FOR FABRIC B

selvage · selvage · 20" · 2½" · 9" · 44"

STEP 2. *sew strips together.*

With right sides facing, pin and sew the long edges of contrasting strips together, alternating prints (i.e., fabric A, B, A, B, etc.). Press the seams open. Mark and cut eight 2½" (6.5cm) strips horizontally across the joined strips. To reinforce the seams, topstitch the long edges of each strip a little less than ¼" (6mm) from the edge.

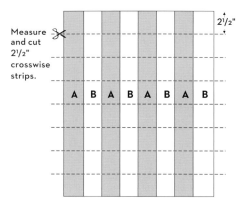

STEP 3. *make the checkerboard.*

Pin the long edges of two strips together with right sides facing, alternating the prints. Sew the strips together along one long edge, aligning the seams as you go. Add the remaining strips in the same way to form the checkerboard. Press all seams open.

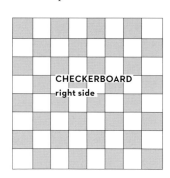

STEP 4. *add felt backing to the checkerboard.*

Center the checkerboard with right side facing the 18" (45.5cm) felt square and align top edges. Pin the layers together. Sew the top edges together. Trim the seam to ⅛" (3mm). Cut away any excess felt on the sides and bottom, even with the checkerboard.

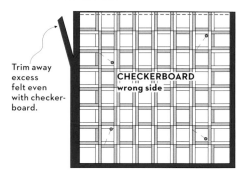

STEP 5. *add the hooked strip to the felt.*

Fold the right side of the checkerboard over the felt so that the right side of the checkerboard is facing out and press flat. Topstitch the top folded-over edge ¼" (6mm) from the seam. Center and topstitch the hooked strip of hook-and-loop tape to the felt at the top edge.

STEP 6. *add the looped strip to the bag.*

Press the top edge of the 18" (45.5cm) square of fabric A to the wrong side by ½" (13mm) and again by ½" (13mm). Topstitch close to the edge. Center and topstitch the looped strip of hook-and-loop tape to the underside of the finished top edge.

STEP 7. *sew the layers together.*

With right sides together, align the top edges of the checkerboard and fabric A. Pin all layers (felt, checkerboard, and fabric) together, and trim away any excess fabric. Sew along the three raw edges, leaving the top open. Trim the seam to $\frac{1}{8}$" (3mm), and clip the corners. Turn the bag right side out and press.

FABRIC A
wrong side

STEP 8. *sew on tie.*

Topstitch the sides and bottom edges. Press the short ends of ribbon or tape under $\frac{1}{4}$" (6mm) twice, and sew across to anchor the folded ends. Sew the middle of the tie to the bottom front edge of the checkerboard using a few back-and-forth stitches.

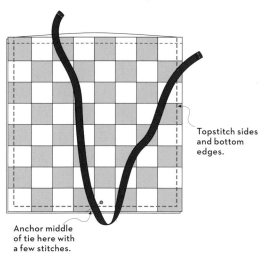

Topstitch sides and bottom edges.

Anchor middle of tie here with a few stitches.

STEP 9. *make reversible checkers.*

Trace the checker template onto cardboard or cardstock and cut it out. From the dark and light solid-color felt, cut out two strips from each color, each $2\frac{1}{4}$" (5.5cm) wide. Place one dark strip on top of a light strip, and pin the circle template on top of the two layers of felt. Sew around the template using a small zigzag stitch; don't sew on the template itself. Cut out the checker close to the stitching using pinking shears or regular scissors. Make the remaining 23 checkers in this way. ***Tip:*** Make a few extra checkers just in case.

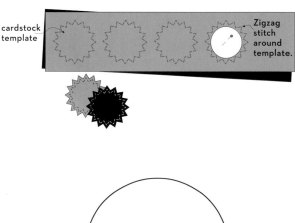

cardstock template

Zigzag stitch around template.

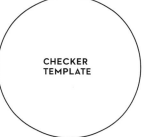

CHECKER TEMPLATE

Modern Shirring
ONE EASY TECHNIQUE, MANY POSSIBILITIES

I love elastic thread. I don't know who invented it, but that person deserves an award.

Shirring—sewing with elastic thread—imitates the beautiful but laborious technique of smocking and magically transforms nonstretch fabric, such as woven cotton, into stretchy fabric. Another big advantage is that it allows for flexibility in fit. This is fantastic for kids' clothes, because they grow so quickly. A garment with a little "give" will fit them for more than one season.

I've provided instructions for three pretty girls' garments that use shirring: two blouses with shirring details and a tiered skirt with a comfy shirred waist. The Lila blouse is a short-sleeved peasant-style blouse with a flared midriff, while the Juliette blouse is a long-sleeved top. Both blouses use the same pattern for the bodice and sleeves. The short-sleeved blouse uses the midriff pattern, but for the long-sleeved tunic, I just lengthened the bodice pattern. Using the same bodice, sleeve, and midriff patterns as the starting point, you can make a blouse or even a dress with long or short sleeves, ruffled or gathered cap sleeves, with or without an empire waist.

These basic shapes and techniques can be combined in many interesting ways that I hope you'll explore. Read through all the tips, and refer back to them before you begin each shirring project. You also may want to practice your shirring first.

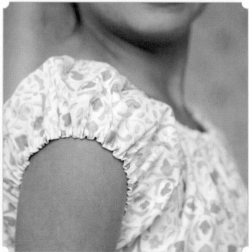

Important Tips for Using Elastic Thread

☙ The elastic thread is used only in the bobbin; don't thread the needle with it.

☙ Wind the bobbin by hand but not too tightly.

☙ Do all your shirring at once so that you don't have to continually change bobbins.

☙ Practice using elastic thread on scrap fabric to figure out the best tension setting for your sewing machine.

☙ Elastic thread can jam up the bobbin more often than regular thread, so you should experiment a bit to find the right tension before starting a project.

☙ Use a straight stitch set at the longest stitch length.

☙ Always sew on the top side of the garment so that the elastic thread is on the underside and doesn't show.

☙ Whenever possible, start and stop sewing at a seam or in an inconspicuous spot.

☙ The more rows of shirring you make, the more stretch you'll get.

☙ Gently stretch the fabric out after the first row of shirring as you sew.

☙ Start and end your stitching by backstitching a couple of times. Then tie the ends of the elastic together in a knot to secure the stitches.

☙ If you're shirring several rows, instead of stopping at the end of each row, just dip down diagonally when you reach the starting point and start a new row.

☙ When you're done shirring, always steam and lightly iron the shirring. This makes it gather a lot more.

Fast and Easy Shirring Projects

terrific tee
Take a T-shirt that's a couple of sizes too big and cut off the neckline band. Trim the sleeves and bottom of the shirt just above the hem. Leaving the edges raw, sew two or three rows of elastic stitches around each opening.

flattering refit
Have a blouse or top that hangs straight and doesn't flatter? Use a few short rows of shirring at the waist on the back to give a more fitted look and to add a decorative detail.

pillowcase sundress
Make a toddler's summer dress or top using a pretty vintage pillowcase. Cut off the short side seam, press the top edge under to get the right length, and trim the folded part to 2" (5cm). Starting at the top sew multiple rows of shirring ¼" (6mm) apart. Shirr all the way down to the waist or just enough for an empire effect. Add straps.

LILA SHIRRED BLOUSE

This blouse is made up of a bodice, sleeves, and midriff. The sleeves can be shirred to make a little cap sleeve or left unshirred for a ruffled sleeve. Use a ¼" (6mm) seam allowance unless the directions specify otherwise.

STEP 1. *cut out the pieces.*

Using the Child's Blouse Sleeve, Bodice, and Midriff patterns, cut out two of each on the fold following the diagram. If you're using one fabric for the bodice and midriff, you can tape the patterns together and cut them out as one piece.

FINISHED MEASUREMENTS

SIZE	CHEST
1/2	21" (53.5cm)
3/4	23" (58.5cm)
5/6	25" (63.5cm)
7/8	27" (68.5cm)
9/10	28½" (72cm)
11/12	30" (76cm)
13/14	32" (81cm)

YARDAGE

One or two 44/45" (112/114cm) cotton prints in the following amounts:

SIZE	1–10	11–14
BODICE & SLEEVES	½ yd (45.5 cm)	1¼ yd (1.1m)
MIDRIFF	½ yd (45.5 cm)	1¼ yd (1.1m)

SUPPLIES

- Child's Blouse Sleeve, Bodice, and Midriff patterns
- Your Sewing Box
- Tape (optional)
- Elastic thread

LILA BLOUSE LAYOUT (1 FABRIC, ALL SIZES)

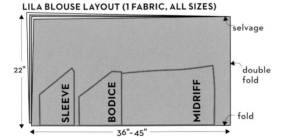

LILA BLOUSE LAYOUT (2 FABRICS, SIZES 11-14)

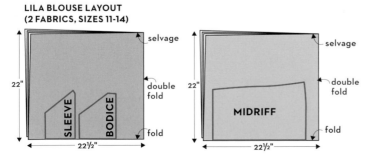

LILA BLOUSE LAYOUT (2 FABRICS, SIZES 2-10)

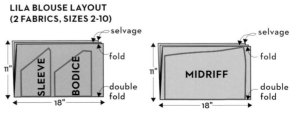

STEP 2. *join the sleeves, bodice, and midriff.*

With right sides together, pin and sew both sleeves to the bodice. With right sides together, pin and sew the midriff sections to the bottom edge of the bodice sections. (Skip this if you taped the patterns together.)

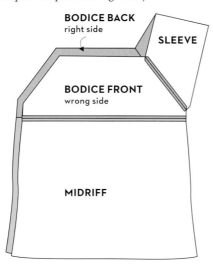

STEP 3. *sew the side seams and finish the hem.*

With right sides facing, pin and sew the side seams together from the sleeve edge to the hem. Press the bottom edge to the inside by 1" (2.5cm), and then press the raw edge under by ¹⁄₂" (13mm). Pin and topstitch close to the edge to finish the hem.

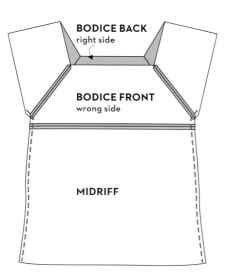

STEP 4. *finish the neck and sleeve edges.*

Using a narrow zigzag stitch with the length set to 1, finish the neck edge very close to the raw edge to help prevent fraying; you can also use a serger. Press the neck edges to the wrong side by ¹⁄₂" (13mm). For a cap sleeve, finish the edges in the same way, and press under by ¹⁄₄" (6mm). For a ruffled sleeve, press the edges under by ¹⁄₄" (6mm) and repeat. Topstitch close to the edge.

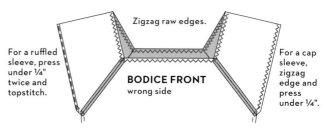

STEP 5. *shirr the neckline.*

Review the tips for shirring (page 74), and then wind your bobbin with elastic thread by hand and set your machine at the longest stitch. Begin stitching at a seam on the right side of the garment, ¹⁄₈" (3mm) from the edge, making sure the edge remains folded under. Begin stitching around the neckline, stopping at the seams to, with the needle down and presser foot lifted, reposition the garment around the corners as needed. Sew two more lines of shirring ¹⁄₄" (6mm) apart. Backstitch a couple of times at the beginning and end of each row, and knot the ends of the elastic threads to each other when you're finished shirring.

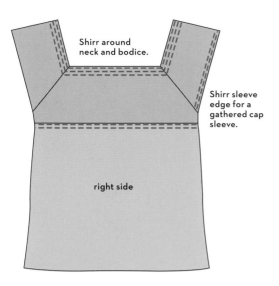

Shirr around neck and bodice.

Shirr sleeve edge for a gathered cap sleeve.

right side

STEP 6. *shirr the bodice.*

Starting at the side seam, shirr the bodice by sewing just under the seam that joins the bodice to the skirt. As you reach the beginning of the seam, dip down diagonally by 1/4" (6mm) and continue shirring (see diagram for Tiered Skirt, step 5 page 86). (If you taped the patterns together, press a horizontal crease 1" [2.5cm] below the bottom of the sleeve, and use this as a guideline for shirring.) Depending on the desired look, you can space the two rows of stitching farther apart, or you can add several more rows of shirring. For the blouse on page 80, I sewed the second row of shirring 1 1/4" (3cm) from the first.

STEP 7. *shirr the sleeves.*

For a gathered cap sleeve, shirr 1/8" (3mm) from the folded edge around the sleeve opening. Make a second row of shirring 1/8" (3mm) from the first row.

JULIETTE SHIRRED BLOUSE

This long-sleeve blouse can be made with woven cotton or two-way stretch cotton knit. If you'd like to use knit but have never sewn with knits before, review the knits section on page 136 before you begin. Use a ¼ " (6mm) seam allowance unless the directions specify otherwise.

STEP 1. *cut out the pieces.*

Using the Child's Blouse Bodice and Sleeve patterns, cut out two of each on the fold, extending the sleeve and bodice to the desired length, as shown in the diagram.

JULIETTE BLOUSE BODICE LAYOUT (LONG SLEEVES, ALL SIZES)

22"

Extend bodice from here. Measure starting 1" from underarm. Add 1" for hem.

BODICE   BODICE

fold

36"–45"

JULIETTE BLOUSE SLEEVE LAYOUT (LONG SLEEVES, ALL SIZES)

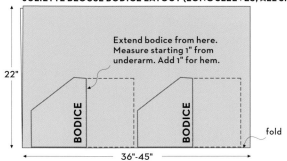

22"

Extend sleeve from here. Measure arm from shoulder and add 3½".

Extend sleeve from here. Measure arm from shoulder and add 3½".

SLEEVE   SLEEVE

fold

36"–45"

FINISHED MEASUREMENTS

SIZE	CHEST
1/2	21" (53.5cm)
3/4	23" (58.5cm)
5/6	25" (63.5cm)
7/8	27" (68.5cm)
9/10	28½" (72cm)
11/12	30" (76cm)
13/14	32" (81cm)

YARDAGE

2 yd (1.8m) of 44/45" (112/114cm) woven cotton print or two-way stretch cotton knit for sizes 1/2, 3/4, 5/6

3 yd (2.3m) of 44/45" (112/114cm) woven cotton print or two-way stretch cotton knit for sizes 7/8, 9/10, 11/12, and 13/14

SUPPLIES

• Child's Blouse Bodice and Sleeve patterns

• Your Sewing Box

• Elastic thread

STEP 2. *join the sleeves and bodice.*

With right sides together, pin and sew the sleeves to the bodice, and then sew the underarm and side seams. If you're using knit fabric, make sure to use a narrow zigzag stitch for this.

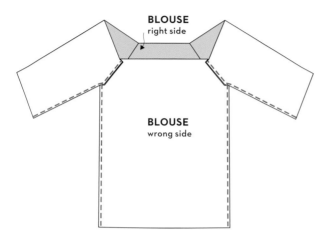

STEP 3. *finish the hem.*

To finish the hem when using woven fabric, press the bottom edge to the inside by ¹⁄₂" (13mm), repeat. Pin and topstitch close to the edge. To finish the hem when using knit fabric, fold (don't press with an iron) the bottom edge to the inside by 1" and pin.

STEP 4. *finish the neckline.*

If using woven fabric, sew the edges of the neckline using a narrow zigzag stitch set to 1 (or a serger) to prevent fraying. Press the edge under by ¹⁄₄" (6mm). Skip this if you're using knit fabric. Instead just fold (don't press with an iron) the raw edge under by ¹⁄₄" and pin.

STEP 5. *shirr the sleeves, hem, and neckline.*

Review the tips for shirring on page 74, wind your bobbin with elastic thread by hand, and set your machine at the longest stitch.

Starting at a seam on the right side (outside) of the garment, sew ¹⁄₈" (3mm) from the folded-under neck edge (use a straight stitch for both woven and knit fabric), making sure the edge remains folded under as you sew. When you reach the next seam, stop, and with the needle down, lift the presser foot, reposition the angle of the garment, and resume sewing. Continue this way, sewing a total of three rows of shirring ¹⁄₄" (6mm) apart. Backstitch a couple of times at the beginning and end of each row, and tie the elastic threads together in a knot when you're finished shirring.

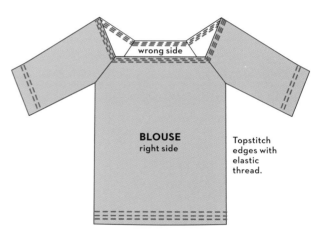

Press (don't press with an iron if using knit fabric, just fold) the bottom sleeve edges to the inside by 1" (2.5cm). Press (don't press with an iron if using knit fabric, just fold and pin) the folded edge to the inside again by 2" (5cm). Starting 1¹⁄₂" (3.8cm) from the folded edge of the sleeve at the seam, sew (using a straight stitch for both woven and knit fabric) two rows of shirring ¹⁄₄" (6mm) apart. Repeat for the other sleeve. Backstitch a couple of times at the beginning and end of each row, and tie the elastic threads together in a knot when you're finished shirring.

Starting at a side seam and using a straight stitch for both woven and knit fabric, shirr the hem by making three rows of shirring but dipping down diagonally by ¹/₄" (6mm) as you approach the starting point so that you're shirring continuously instead of stopping at the end of each row (see diagram for Tiered Skirt, step 5, page 86). Finish the shirring as instructed above.

TIERED SKIRT

This tiered skirt has a wonderful full, flowing feel that can be made to any size. The basic technique can be used to make a sundress, as well. Use a ¼" (6mm) seam allowance unless the directions specify otherwise.

STEP 1. *measure and cut.*

Measure your child around the lower waist, and decide how long you want the skirt to be. Write down the length and waist measurements. To determine the length of each tier, divide the desired length by 3; we'll call this number A. Then the tier lengths are as follows:

First tier: A + $2\frac{1}{4}$" (5.5cm)

Second tier: A + $\frac{1}{2}$" (13mm)

Third tier: A + $2\frac{1}{4}$" (5.5cm)

To determine the width of each tier, divide the waist measurement by 2; we'll call this number B.

First tier: B + 5" (12.5cm); round the amount to the nearest $\frac{1}{4}$" (6mm)

Second tier: [B + 5" (12.5cm)] x 1.5; round the amount to the nearest $\frac{1}{4}$" (6mm)

Third tier: [B + 5" (12.5cm)] x 1.5 x 1.5; round the amount to the nearest $\frac{1}{4}$" (6mm)

Cut two of each tier using the measurements you just calculated for the length and width of each one.

STEP 2. *gather and sew the tiers.*

With right sides together, sew each pair of tiers together along the short sides to make three loops.

Sew the upper edge of the third tier $\frac{1}{4}$" (6mm) from the edge using a long basting stitch; don't lock the stitches at the beginning or end. Gently pull just one thread to gather the third tier until it is the same width as the second tier. In the same way, gather the second tier until it is the same width as the first tier.

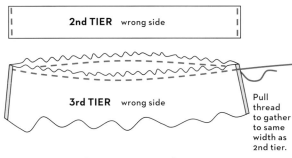

STEP 3. *join the tiers together.*

Place the second-tier loop inside the third tier with right sides together. Align the gathered edge of the third tier with the bottom edge of the second tier, and align the side seams. Pin and sew the edges together. Repeat this procedure to join the second tier to the first tier. Press all seams up without flattening the gathers.

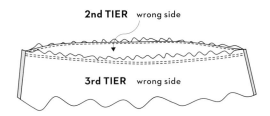

STEP 4. *hem the skirt.*

Press the bottom edge of the skirt under by 1" (2.5cm); repeat. Pin and topstitch close to the edge to make the hem.

STEP 5. *shirr the waistline.*

Press the top of the skirt under by $2\frac{1}{2}$" (5cm), and then press the raw edge under by $\frac{1}{2}$" (13mm) and pin. Review and follow the tips for shirring (page 74), and then wind your bobbin with elastic thread by hand, and set your machine at the longest stitch.

Starting at the side seam on the outside of the skirt, topstitch $\frac{1}{8}$" (3mm) from the top edge, dipping down diagonally by $\frac{1}{4}$" (6mm) when you approach the starting point. In this way, sew four continuous rows of elastic $\frac{1}{4}$" (6mm) apart.

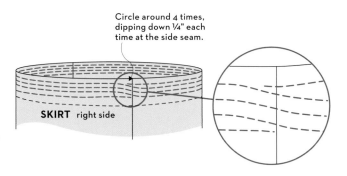

Set your iron to steam, and lightly press the elastic stitching to make the elastic gather up fully. Backstitch a couple of times at the beginning and end of each stitch line; then tie the ends of the elastic threads together in a knot.

As an alternative you can make each tier out of smaller bits of fabric pieced together. Make sure to add $\frac{1}{2}$" (13mm) to each piece for the seam allowance. This skirt can be made as a dress by making each tier longer and, instead of measuring the child around the waist, measuring around the chest under the arms and then following the directions for the skirt. Instead of four rows of shirring, continue shirring the entire top tier. Sew two pieces of ribbon to the inside top edge to make a simple halter that ties around the neck.

03

HOME
STYLE

Sewing is a wonderful and economical way to express your personal style sense in your home. There are many fabulous modern fabrics that can be found fairly inexpensively. In the past, medium-weight cotton fabrics were designed and used mostly for quilting, while more expensive upholstery-weight fabrics with their larger design motifs were the only option for home decor projects. These days, the easy availability and incredible selection of cotton "quilting" fabrics in vibrant colors and large patterns make them a wonderful option for the home. I used cotton quilting fabric for all the projects in this chapter, because they're less expensive and more easily washable than upholstery fabric, which may require dry cleaning.

These projects are easy and extremely useful. Purely decorative items have their place, of course, but I prefer to make things that are both beautiful and useful. The big Apple Pie Ottoman is great for sitting on, the Pincushions are a bright way of keeping your needles within easy reach, and the Soft Fabric Shade makes a practical and inexpensive custom window dressing.

APPLE PIE OTTOMAN

I could be very happy in a sunny white room with nothing but huge printed pillows for decoration. Pretty and practical, this ottoman is supereasy, and it's a good way to use up the smaller pieces of fabric in your stash. The pieced cover can be removed for washing. For more interest, try cutting the wedges from fabric that has already been pieced. You can make this ottoman to any size by redrawing the curved edge of the pattern piece farther inside for a smaller pillow or extending the curved edge of the pattern piece outward for a larger one. Use a ¼" (6mm) seam allowance unless the directions specify otherwise.

FINISHED MEASUREMENTS
24" wide x 6½" high (61cm x 16.5cm)

YARDAGE
2 yd (1.8m) of 44/45" (112/114cm) cotton print for pillow wedges, bottom, and sides (fabric A)

½ yd (45.5cm) of 44/45" (112/114cm) cotton print for pillow wedges (fabric B)

2¼ yd (2m) of 44/45" (112/114cm) muslin for pillow insert

SUPPLIES
• Apple Pie Wedge pattern

• Your Sewing Box

• Two 32-oz (907g) bags of polyester fiberfill

STEP 1. *cut out the wedges.*

Cut fabric A into two 1-yd (91cm) pieces, and set one piece aside. Using the Apple Pie Wedge pattern, cut out four wedges and two 7½" x 40" (19cm x 101.5cm) side strips from fabric A. From fabric B, cut out four wedges.

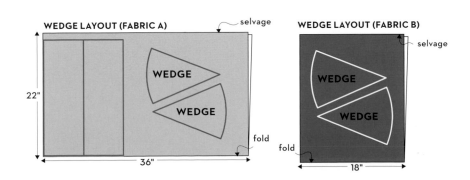

WEDGE LAYOUT (FABRIC A) — selvage — 22" — 36" — fold — WEDGE — WEDGE

WEDGE LAYOUT (FABRIC B) — selvage — fold — 18" — WEDGE — WEDGE

STEP 2. *make the cover top.*

With right sides facing and alternating prints, sew four wedges together along their straight edges, pressing the seam open after adding each wedge, to form a half circle. Make another half circle with the four remaining wedges. Trim off the points in the center of the seam. With right sides facing, align the straight edges and centers of the half circles, and sew along the edge in a straight line (this will avoid puckering in the middle).

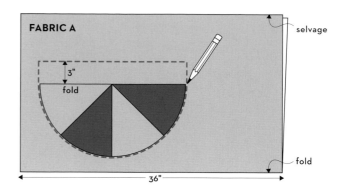

STEP 3. *make the muslin insert.*

Using the completed top as a template, cut two circles and two 7½" x 40" (19cm x 101.5cm) strips from muslin. Sew the muslin strips together along a short edge to make one long strip.

Mark, fold, and press one raw end under by 2" (5cm). Starting at the fold, with right sides together, align the long edge of the strip and the edge of one muslin circle, and sew all the way around, allowing the raw end to overlap. Sew the opposite long edge of the strip to the second muslin circle in the same way. Turn right side out, stuff with fiber-fill, and whipstitch the opening closed.

STEP 4. *cut out the cover bottom.*

Fold the finished pillow top in half, and place on top of the folded fabric A piece you set aside earlier. Trace around the curve onto fabric A. Measure 3" (7.5cm) above the middle of the pillow top, and draw a straight line across. Cut out the two (oversized) half circles. On both pieces, press the straight edge under by ½" (13mm) and repeat. Topstitch to finish the edges.

STEP 5. *sew the bottom sections together.*

Lay both halves of the bottom sections on the pillow top, wrong sides facing down, aligning curved edges and overlapping the straight edges so that they fit the circle. Pin the two bottom sections together, and sew close to the topstitching for 3" (7.5cm) from the edge toward the center on both sides, leaving a large opening to insert the muslin pillow.

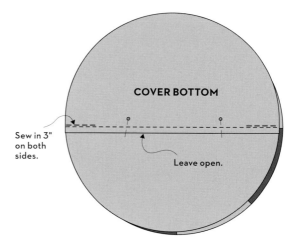

STEP 6. *assemble the slipcover.*

Sew two fabric A strips, right sides together, along one short side. Mark, fold, and press one end under 2" (5cm), and sew the strip to the top and bottom cover, as you did with the muslin in step 3. Whipstitch the side edges closed. Turn right side out, and insert the muslin pillow.

TWO PRETTY
PINCUSHIONS

TWO PRETTY PINCUSHIONS

Sewers cannot have too many pincushions. Along with the ones on my ironing board and by my sewing machine, TV chair, and cutting table, I have extras piled on a cake plate and in a basket because they're just plain pretty. Friends love getting these as gifts, and they are a good way to use up your leftover fabrics. Here are directions for two pretty pincushions that are quick and easy to make. The Pieced Pincushion is a simple patchwork "pinnie" that gets its personality from the placement of the prints. The Pretty Posy pinnie is like a little flower with its frilly, topstitched edge. It can be made bigger by extending the curved edge of the wedge pattern outward. You could also enlarge the patterns and make pillows or add hanging loops and make sweet holiday ornaments. Use a ¼" (6mm) seam allowance unless the directions specify otherwise.

FINISHED MEASUREMENTS
6½" (16.5cm) square

YARDAGE
Scraps of two contrasting cotton prints for the top

7" (18cm) square of cotton fabric for the bottom

SUPPLIES
• Your Sewing Box

• 2 oz (57g) of polyester fiberfill

• ½ yd (45.5cm) of size 10 crochet cotton

• One ⅝" to ⅞" button

PIECED PINCUSHION

STEP 1. *cut out the triangles.*

From each fabric, cut two 4" (10cm) squares. Cut the squares in half on the diagonal to form eight triangles. Lay out the triangles to create the desired pattern.

STEP 2. *sew the triangles together.*

With right sides facing, sew the diagonal edges of two triangles together. Press the seams open, and trim off the points even with the edge of the square. Repeat with the other three pairs of triangles.

STEP 3. *sew the squares together.*

With right sides facing, sew the two top squares together to form the top row. Repeat with the two bottom squares to form the bottom row. Press the seams open. Sew the rows together to form the pincushion top. Press the middle seam open.

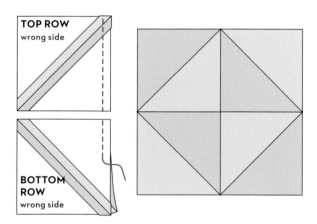

STEP 4. *sew the top and bottom together.*

With right sides together, pin the top to the 7" (18cm) square. Sew all around, leaving a 3" (7.5cm) opening. Trim the corners, and turn right side out. Stuff the pincushion tight, and whipstitch the opening closed.

STEP 5. *tie the pincushion.*

Thread the crochet cotton through a needle, and knot one strand. Poke the needle through the center bottom, leaving a 6" (15cm) tail, and up through the top center and through one button hole. Poke the needle down through the other button hole to the bottom center. Pull the thread tight enough to make an indent in the pincushion, and repeat again, pulling the thread tight. Take a couple of stitches in the bottom center to anchor the threads. Work the needle through a few threads, and tie the thread ends together a couple of times in a knot. Cut the thread close to the pincushion.

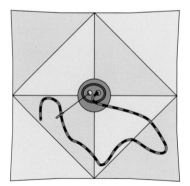

PRETTY POSY PINCUSHION

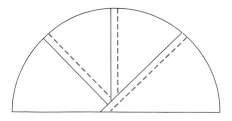

FINISHED MEASUREMENTS
5½" (14cm) diameter

YARDAGE
Scraps of contrasting cotton prints for top

7" (18cm) square of cotton fabric for bottom

SUPPLIES
• Posy Pincushion Wedge pattern

• Your Sewing Box

• 2 oz (57g) of polyester fiberfill

STEP 1. *cut out the wedges.*

Using the Posy Wedge template (opposite), cut out a total of eight wedges in desired fabrics for the top of the pincushion.

STEP 2. *sew the wedges together.*

With right sides facing, sew two wedges together along one side. Add the third and fourth wedges, forming a semicircle. Snip off the points flush with the straight edge. Make another semicircle with the four remaining wedges.

STEP 3. *sew the semicircles together.*

With right sides facing, align the straight edges of the semicircles, matching the centers. Sew the straight edges together, but leave a 2" (5cm) opening for turning. Press the middle seam open.

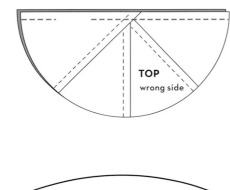

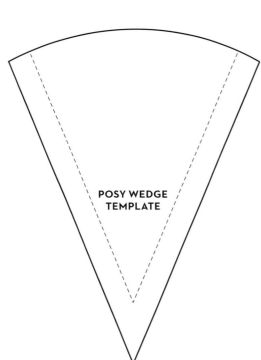

POSY WEDGE
TEMPLATE

STEP 4. *join the top and bottom.*

Pin the circle onto the middle of the 7" (18cm) square, right sides together, and sew all around ¼" (6mm) from the edge of the circle.

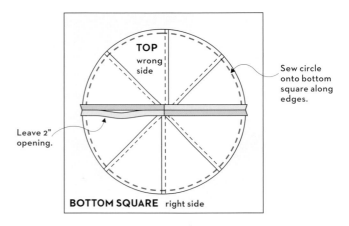

STEP 5. *topstitch the edges.*

Turn the pincushion right side out and press. Make three or four rows (the more rows of topstitching, the more ruffled the edge will be) of topstitching around the pincushion, starting ⅛" (3mm) from the edge and spaced ⅛" (3mm) apart. Stuff with fiberfill until the pincushion is firm. Whipstitch the opening closed.

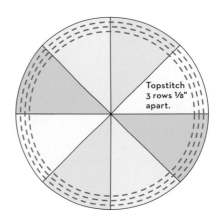

EASY REVERSIBLE FABRIC BOX OR TOTE

This is my absolute favorite method of making a fabric box or tote, because it is easy, intuitive, allows for a mix of fabrics, and can be made in any size. It uses the same technique as the Soft Baby Blocks (page 67), and it can be easily adapted to make big stuffed square cushions. Make little boxes to hold odds and ends on your work and sewing surfaces, or add a handle to create a storage tote. See the baby blocks directions for more ideas. These instructions are for boxes in three different sizes. Use a ¼" (6mm) seam allowance unless the directions specify otherwise.

FINISHED MEASUREMENTS
Small box: 6" (15cm) wide x 6" (15cm) high x 6" (15cm) deep

Medium box: 8" (20.5cm) wide x 8" (20.5cm) high x 8" (20.5cm) deep

Large box: 10" (25.5cm) wide x 10" (25.5cm) high x 10" (25.5cm) deep

YARDAGE
⅓ yd (½ yd, ½ yd) (30.5cm [45.5cm, 45.5cm]) of 44/45" (112/114cm) cotton print for box exterior (fabric A)

⅓ yd (½ yd, ½ yd) (30.5cm [45.5cm, 45.5cm]) of 44/45" (112/114cm) cotton print or heavy-weight cotton for lining (fabric B)

⅝ yd (¾ yd, 1 yd) (57cm [68.5cm, 91cm]) of sew-in interfacing. Interfacing is optional if you use heavy-weight canvas for fabric B. For a more flexible box, use a medium- to heavy-weight Peltex or equivalent or, for a stiffer box, use Peltex 70 Ultra Firm Stabilizer or equivalent

SUPPLIES
- Your Sewing Box
- 2 or 3 sheets of 8½" x 11" (21.5cm x 28cm) paper, long sides taped together
- 30" (76cm) length of 1" (2.5cm) cotton webbing or belting, cut in half to make two 15" (38cm) handles (optional)

STEP 1. *make the paper pattern.*
Draw two identical-size squares on your paper, one above the other, in the dimension of the finished box—6", 8", or 10" (15cm, 20.5cm, or 25.5cm)—plus ½" (13mm) in total for the seam allowance (6½", 8½", or 10½") [16.5cm., 21.5cm, or 26.5cm]. Use a magazine, book, or piece of paper to make sure all corners are 90 degrees. Inside the bottom square, draw a diagonal line from one corner to the opposite corner. Repeat with the two remaining corners, forming an X. Cut out the top square and attached triangle as one piece. This is your pattern.

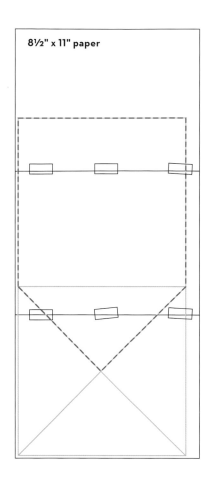

8½" x 11" paper

STEP 2. *cut out the pieces.*

Using your pattern, cut four pieces from fabric A and four pieces from fabric B. If using interfacing, cut out four pieces, and pin them to the wrong side of the fabric A pieces and skip to step 3.

If using ultrafirm stabilizer, cut out four pieces for the sides of the box in the following dimensions (length x width):

Small box: 6⅜" x 5⅞" (16cm x 14.7cm)
Medium box: 8⅜" x 7⅞" (21.5cm x 20.2cm)
Large box: 10⅜" x 9⅞" (26.5cm x 25.2cm)

For the bottom of the box, cut one square of stabilizer in the same dimensions as the final box: 6" (15cm), 8" (20.5cm), or 10" (25.5 cm).

STEP 3. *sew the box.*

With right sides together, sew together two fabric A pieces along one straight side and one slope of the triangle. Join the two remaining pieces in the same way. To form the box, sew these two halves, with right sides together, down one side, along the bottom, and up the other side. Repeat with the lining (fabric B) pieces.

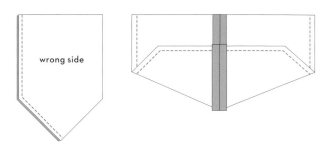

wrong side

STEP 4. *add the ultrafirm stabilizer.*

If you're not using ultrafirm stabilizer, skip to step 5.

Pin the shorter edge of the stabilizer side pieces to the inside walls of the box, centering each between the corner seams and aligning them at the top. Baste along the top, ½" (13mm) from the edge. Place the stabilizer square at the bottom of the cube.

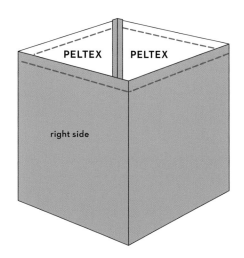

PELTEX   PELTEX

right side

STEP 5. *add handles (optional).*

To omit the handles, skip to step 6.

On two opposite sides of the box, mark lightly with a pencil where you want the handles to go, spacing them evenly. Align the side edge of the handle at these marks, positioning the raw ends 2" (5cm) above the top box edge, and anchor each handle with a few stitches.

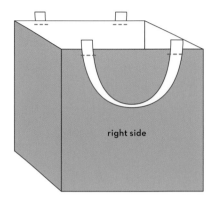

right side

STEP 6. *join the box and lining.*

Place the cube inside the lining, with right sides facing and the top edges aligned. Sew around the edge, leaving one side open. Carefully turn the box right side out, and arrange to form a box with a lining. Press along the top of the box to get a crisp edge. Press the raw edges under, even with the top. Topstitch ¼" (6mm) from the edge. Topstitch an X over each handle to secure it well.

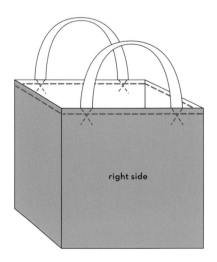

right side

DOROTHY APRON

This apron style is a celebration of the 1920s and '30s, apple crisp, lemonade, and red-and-white kitchens—all the nostalgia of a simpler time. With dressmaker pleated details and a ruffle, it is definitely a girly-girl apron and would look great made in either a vintage-looking fabric or something with a more modern feel. Use a ¼" (6mm) seam allowance unless the directions specify otherwise.

FINISHED MEASUREMENTS
Length from top of bib to bottom of hem: 31" (79cm)

Width across bust: 27½" (70cm)

Width across hem: 36" (91cm)

YARDAGE
1½ yd (1.4m) of 44/45" (112/114cm) cotton print

SUPPLIES
• Dorothy Apron and Pocket patterns

• Your Sewing Box

• Washable pencil

STEP 1. *cut out the pieces.*

Using the Dorothy Apron and Pocket patterns, pin the patterns to the fabric, and cut out one apron and two pockets (optional). Also measure and cut one 12" x 36" (30.5cm x 91cm) rectangle on the fold for the facing, one 4½" x 44" (11.5cm x 112cm) ruffle, and two 2½" x 44" (6.5cm x 112cm) straps, as shown.

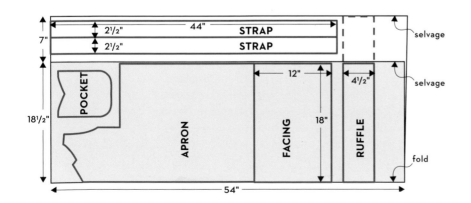

STEP 2. *make the pleats.*

Transfer the pleat marks (dots) from the paper pattern to the right side of the apron with a washable pencil. Make the side pleats by folding the apron with right sides together and aligning the top and bottom dots. Press the pleats on the wrong side of the apron to get a crisp fold and pin. Sew between the dots ³⁄₄" (2cm) from the folded edge of the pleat on the wrong side of the apron. Make the center front pleats in the same way, lining them up smoothly at the neckline. Press the pleats away from the center on the wrong side of the apron.

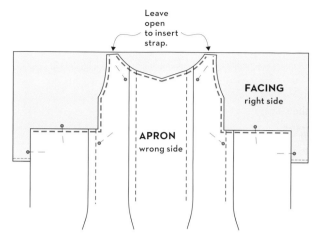

STEP 3. *attach the facing.*

Press the long bottom edge of the facing rectangle to the wrong side by ¹⁄₄" (6mm), and repeat to make a hem for the facing. Topstitch close to the edge. Place the facing on a flat surface, right side up. Center the top portion of the apron, right side down, on top of the facing, and pin the layers together. Sew around the top edges of the apron, leaving the sides and the two openings for the straps unsewn. Trim the facing even with the apron. Clip the curves and corners.

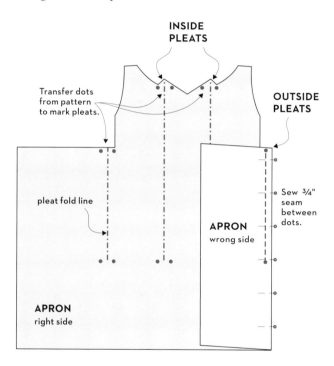

STEP 4. *make and attach the straps.*

Cut the straps in half so that they are each 22" (56cm) long by 2¹⁄₂" (6.5cm) wide. Fold each strap in half lengthwise, with right sides facing. Pin and sew the long edges. Use a safety pin to turn the straps right side out and press. If you've never done this before, pin a safety pin to the opening at one end, and then insert the head of the pin into the same opening it's pinned to. Gather the fabric along the pin, and pull it backward until the pin comes out the other side and the strap is turned right side out. Insert the straps in between the apron and facing, aligning each raw edge with a strap opening. Sew through the facing, strap, and apron to attach the strap. Repeat with the second strap. Turn the apron and facing right side out and press well. Press the raw edges of the ends of both straps to the inside by ¹⁄₄" (6mm); press and topstitch ends.

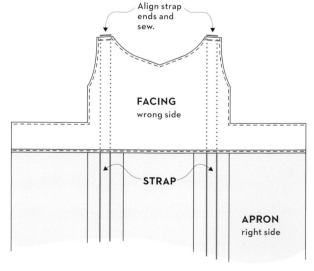

STEP 5. *finish the sides and attach side straps.*

Fold the raw edges of the apron sides under by ¹/₄" (6mm) and press; repeat and topstitch close to the edge to finish the sides. Press the raw ends of the straps to the inside ¹/₄" (6mm), and topstitch closed. Sew the end of the strap to the wrong side of the apron at the waist, making a neat square and backstitching to anchor threads.

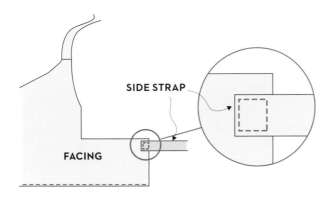

STEP 6. *make the ruffle.*

Fold the ruffle lengthwise with right sides facing. Sew together along both short ends. Turn the ruffle right side out, and press flat. Without backstitching at the beginning or end, sew a row of long basting stitches ¹/₈" (3mm) from the raw edge. Pull just one thread, and gently gather the ruffle along the thread until it is the same width as the bottom of the apron. Align and pin the raw edge of the ruffle to the right side of the skirt bottom edge and sew. Fold up the seam allowance and press flat.

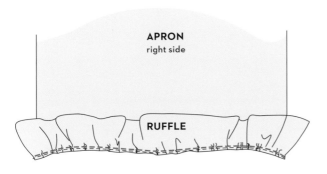

STEP 7. *make and attach the pocket (optional).*

With right sides facing, sew the top, sides, and bottom of the pockets together, leaving a 2" (5cm) opening along one side. Clip curves. Turn right side out and press. Fold and press the opening at the side of the pocket to the inside ¹/₄" (6mm) and press. Pin the pocket to the apron where desired. Topstitch the sides and bottom ¹/₈" (3mm) from the edge.

SOFT FABRIC SHADE

Fabric shades are an economical way to stylishly cover windows of any size. Let your style show through your fabric choices. Use one fabric for the front, or piece together as many fabrics as you like for a quilt-top effect. You can make this shade soft and casual, or use a light-weight wooden dowel, available in hardware and crafts stores, in the top and/or bottom to give it a little more structure. You need just two cup hooks to mount the shade—this makes it a great alternative for rentals, as there are only two little holes to spackle when you move. Use a ¼" (6mm) seam allowance unless the directions specify otherwise.

FINISHED DIMENSIONS
Depends on your window size

YARDAGE
One or more cotton fabrics for the shade (See step 1 to determine yardage/dimensions.)

White or light-color muslin or sheeting for the backing (See step 1 to determine yardage/dimensions.)

SUPPLIES
- Your Sewing Box

- ⅛" (3mm) nylon or cotton cording (nylon slides more easily) (See step 1 to determine yardage/dimensions.)

- 2¼" (5.5cm) wooden dowels, available through craft and hardware stores, cut 1½" (3.8cm) smaller than the width of your finished shade (optional) (See step 1 to determine yardage/dimensions.)

- ½ yd (45.5cm) of ½" (13mm) cotton twill tape, cut into ten 1¾" (4.5cm) pieces

- 2 medium-size cup hooks

STEP 1. *calculate the yardages.*

Decide if you want to mount the shade on the molding or inside the window frame so that the molding is not obscured. Either way, measure the entire area you plan to cover. Add ½" (13mm) to the length and to the width, and write the dimensions here: length =___; width =___. Using these dimensions, figure out and write down how much you'll need of the following:

Cording: Cut two pieces, one longer than the other. The shorter cord is the length measurement plus 4" (10cm) = ___ ; the longer cord is the length plus width plus 4" (10cm) = ___.

Dowels (optional): Cut two dowels, each equal to the width minus 1½" (3.8cm) = ___.

Shade Backing: Cut one rectangle equal to the length and width you determined earlier = ___.

Shade Front: Cut one rectangle equal to the length and width you determined earlier = ___. (For a pieced shade, see step 2.)

STEP 2. *piece the shade front (optional).*

Instead of using one fabric for the shade front, for a more exciting effect you may want to sew strips or squares of fabric together in a crazy-quilt or checkerboard pattern, or make horizontal, diagonal, or vertical stripes. Use a $\frac{1}{4}$" (6mm) seam allowance when sewing the pieces together, and press all seams open. Trim the pieced shade to the dimensions you calculated in step 1.

STEP 3. *attach the twill tape tabs.*

Position the twill tape tabs on the backing $1\frac{1}{2}$" (3.8cm) down from the top and bottom edges and $\frac{1}{2}$" (13mm) in from each side. Sew the tabs to the backing $\frac{1}{4}$" (6mm) from the tab edges, sewing forward and backstitching to secure each tab well. Sew three more tabs down each side, spacing them evenly.

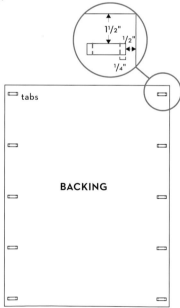

STEP 4. *sew the shade and backing together.*

With the right side of the shade facing the tabbed side of the backing, pin and sew all four sides, leaving a 6" (15cm) opening at top center. Trim the corners, turn right side out, and push out the corners with the eraser end of a pencil. Press the shade flat.

STEP 5. *insert the dowels (optional).*

If you want the shade to be straight across at the top and bottom, which makes for a more tailored look, insert the two dowels through the opening.

STEP 6. *topstitch the shade.*

Whipstitch the top opening closed. Topstitch all around the shade, $\frac{1}{4}$" (6mm) from the edge, keeping the dowels out of the way. When you're done topstitching, if you're using dowels, move one dowel to the bottom and topstitch 1" (2.5cm) from the bottom edge across the width of the shade. Repeat for the top dowel.

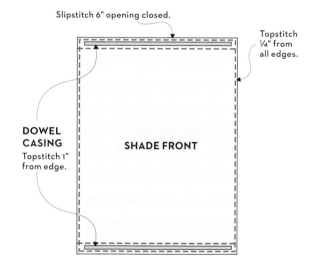

STEP 7. *attach the cords.*

Lay the shade right side down with the tabs facing you. Tie the longer cord (using a double knot) to the bottom tab on the side opposite the one you want the cord to hang from when the shade is facing out. Thread the cord up through the tabs to the top and then over through the opposite top tab, and let it hang down. Next, tie the shorter cord to the other bottom tab, and thread it up through the tabs on that side. Let it hang down from the top.

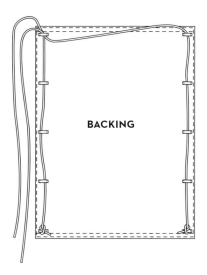

BACKING

STEP 8. *hang the shade.*

Make a pencil mark at the middle of the window frame (inside or outside). Next, measure the distance between the inner edges of the top two tabs on the shade and add 1" (2.5cm). Divide this number in half. Measure and mark this distance from the middle pencil mark you made. Screw the cup hooks in at these marks by hand. Hang the shade on the cup hooks from the top two tabs, making sure both cords are also positioned over the cup hooks. The hooks serve as a batten, providing necessary support when pulling the cords.

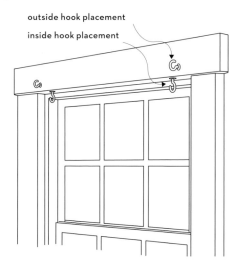

outside hook placement

inside hook placement

STEP 9. *secure the cords.*

When the shade is up, secure the cords by wrapping them around the nearest cup hook, or install another cup hook on the side of the frame to wrap the cords around.

IMPORTANT SAFETY NOTE

Window shades with cords pose a very real strangulation risk to small children. Never use these shades where they can be accessed by little ones. Always anchor cords safely out of the way.

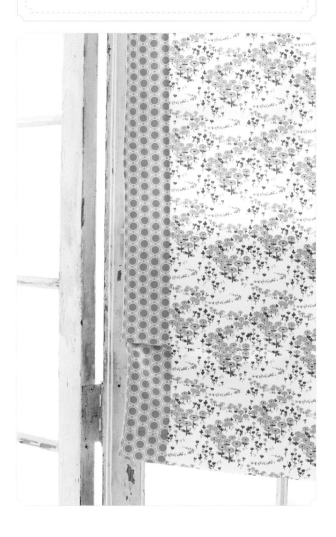

DESIGN-AS-YOU-GO QUILT

If you want to invest weeks or months making a quilt that uses intricate piecing and precision stitching, this is not the quilt for you. This quilt is designed to be made in one or two long and lazy afternoons and is all about your aesthetic and instinct. It uses large rectangles of cotton prints, randomly assembled into strips. The finished quilt is machine-tacked to keep the batting in place. Simply stated, you can't make a mistake with this quilt. You make it right on your bed, designing and editing it as you go. The yardage for your quilt depends on the desired size, on the number of prints you want to use, and in what proportions. The quilt shown uses eight coordinating cotton prints and solids. This quilt was designed and the instructions written by my wonderful mother, Linda Whelan. Use a ½" (13mm) seam allowance unless the directions specify otherwise.

STEP 1. *cut out the strips.*

Measure your mattress, and decide whether you'll use three or five strips. Divide the mattress width by the number of strips, and add 1" (2.5cm) to each to determine the width of each strip. Cut your fabrics into strips in this width using the yardstick, rotary cutter, and self-healing mat (if using).

FINISHED MEASUREMENTS

As desired, depending on the size of the mattress and how much overhang (border) you want on each side.

YARDAGE

Estimates are given below for total yardages of 44/45" (112/114cm) fabric for common mattress sizes:

	CRIB	TWIN	DOUBLE	QUEEN
Center strips*	1½ yd (1.4m)	3 yd (2.7m)	3½ yd (3.2m)	4 yd (3.7m)
Inside border	¼ yd (23cm)	⅜ yd (34.5cm)	½ yd (45.5cm)	½ yd (45.5cm)
Outside border*	1¼ yd (1.1m)	1⅝ yd (1.5m)	1⅞ yd (1.7m)	2 yd (1.8m)

*Represents total yardage for all pieced strips

The quilt backing should be a couple of inches wider all around than your final quilt top. Quilt backing comes in various standard widths, or you can piece it from 44/45" (112/114cm) cotton prints or solids as desired. For assistance, confer with your fabric supplier.

SUPPLIES

- Your Sewing Box

- Yardstick, quilters rule, or other straight edge at least 24" (61cm) long

- Rotary cutter and self-healing mat (optional)

- A piece of cardboard or stiff interfacing at least as wide and as long as the width of each strip (see step 1)

- Quilt batting or fleece in the desired size. If the fleece does not come wide enough, loosely hand-sew the pieces together without overlapping them.

- Quilting pins

- Erasable or washable quilt-marking pencil

(Alternatively, draw straight lines with a pencil and yard-stick and cut the strips with a scissor.) The full-size quilt shown uses five 13" (33cm) strips.

STEP 2. *cut the strips into smaller pieces.*

Cut horizontally across the strips to make smaller rectangles of varying sizes, keeping all the corners nice and square and the widths uniform. The quilt shown uses pieces from 5" to 14" (12.5cm–35.5cm) long.

STEP 3. *create your design.*

Lay all the rectangles out on your bed, forming the desired number of strips, starting in the middle and distributing patterns and colors throughout the quilt. Stand back every so often to get a sense of your total design. Move the pieces around until you're happy with the arrangement.

Starting with any strip, sew the top rectangle to the one beneath it, with right sides together, using a ¹/₂" (13mm) seam. Continue adding rectangles until the strip is the same length as your mattress. Press the seams open. Make the remaining strips. Lay out the strips on your bed every so often so that you can see how it's going and make any desired changes.

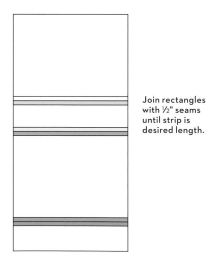

Join rectangles with ½" seams until strip is desired length.

STEP 4. *join the strips together.*

When you're satisfied with your design, align the bottom edges of the strips. With right sides together, sew the long edges of the first and second strips together starting at the bottom and ending at the top, using a ¹/₂" (13mm) seam.

Continue adding strips, sewing from bottom to top until all the strips have been added. Press all seams open. Trim off any excess from the top edge so that it's even and straight across and parallel with the bottom.

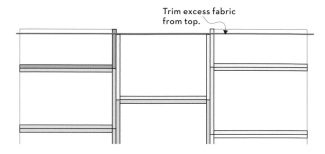

Trim excess fabric from top.

STEP 5. *add the inside border.*

From the inside border fabric, cut a few 2" (5cm) strips (these can be cut either crosswise or lengthwise), and sew the short ends together with right sides facing until the strip is as long as the width of the quilt. Press the seams open. Sew the long edge of the strip to the top of the quilt with right sides together, and trim short edges as needed so the strip is flush with the sides of the quilt. Cut, piece, and sew a second strip to the bottom of the quilt in the same way. Repeat the procedure to make the inside borders for the sides. With right sides together, sew them to each side of the quilt starting at the top border, down the side, to the bottom border, and trim excess so the side borders are flush with the top and bottom borders.

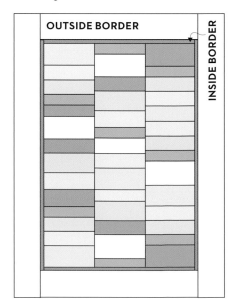

OUTSIDE BORDER

INSIDE BORDER

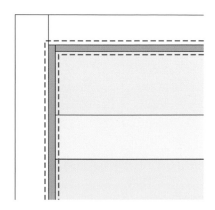

STEP 6. *add the outside border.*

From the outside border fabric, cut several 9" (23cm) strips (or any width as desired), and repeat the procedure in step 5 to add an outside border first to the top and bottom, and then to the sides of the quilt.

STEP 7. *layer the quilt with the batting and backing.*

Place the batting or fleece on a flat surface with the backing piece on top, right side facing up. Center the quilt top, right side facing down, on top of the backing, and smooth out the three layers with your hand. Using the quilting pins, pin all the layers together in strategic places, starting in the middle and continuing to smooth it all out as you go.

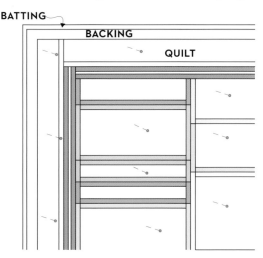

Trim the backing and batting so they are an inch (2.5cm) or so larger than the quilt all around. Keeping the quilt on top and using a ¹/₂" (13mm) seam allowance from the edge of the quilt, sew around the edge of the three layers, leaving a 20" (51cm) opening for turning. Trim excess backing and batting to the same size as the quilt.

Remove the pins and turn the quilt right side out, keeping the batting inside. Fold the edges of the opening to the inside by ¹/₂", pin, and whipstitch the opening closed. Topstitch through all the layers very close to (almost but not quite on top of) the seams that attach the inside and outside borders, all the way around; this is known as *stitch in the ditch.*

STEP 8. *make a tacking template.*

Place your quilt on a flat surface, and measure the width of the finished strips. From the cardboard or interfacing, cut a square in the dimension of the width of the quilt strip. Using a pencil, draw a horizontal and vertical line across the middle of the square, creating a grid of four equal-size squares. Cut a small hole in the middle of the grid using a scissor or other sharp implement (this can be rough). This is your template to use for pinning the quilt where you will tack it.

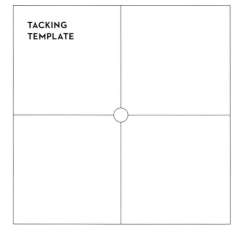

STEP 9. *mark the quilt.*

Place the quilt on a flat surface with the top facing up, and smooth it out with your hands. Using the yardstick, find the vertical and horizontal center of the middle strip, and insert a pin there pointing up (toward the top of the quilt). Place the hole in your template over the center pin.

Holding the template in place, insert a pin (pointing up) into the quilt (not in the template) at each corner of the template, through the middle hole and where the pencil lines meet the fabric. Repeat this process, moving the template up and down the middle strip, and continue to pin—first through the template hole, then at the corners and pencil lines—until you have three vertical lines of evenly spaced pins, all facing up. Do not pin the border, as it will not be tacked.

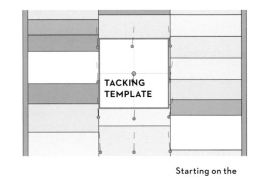

Starting on the middle strip, create 3 vertical lines of evenly spaced pins.

STEP 10. *machine-tack the middle strip.*

You're ready to start machine-tacking. Set a zigzag stitch length at 0 and the width at 4 or 5. You'll start machine-tacking on the middle strip, so you'll need to roll up the right side of the quilt and use safety pins as needed to keep the excess fabric out of the way.

Starting at the top of one of the pinned vertical rows in the middle strip, poke the needle down through the quilt where you inserted your first pin, without removing the pin. Make eight or ten horizontal stitches (tacks) in place right over the pin; don't sew on top of the pin itself or your needle may break. Remove the pin. Without cutting the threads, move down to the next pin and repeat. Continue

on down to the bottom of the row, and then clip off the threads flush with the quilt on both sides. Repeat this procedure for the other two vertical rows on the middle strip, always starting at the top and ending at the bottom.

Following step 9, pin the vertical rows on the strip to the right of middle using your template, and then tack each row from top to bottom, remove pins, and cut threads as described above. Continue this way, tacking one strip at a time, unrolling the quilt as you move to the sides. When you're ready to tack the strips on the left side of center, turn the quilt upside down and repeat the process.

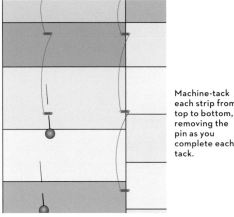

Machine-tack each strip from top to bottom, removing the pin as you complete each tack.

DESIGN GUIDELINES

Color

For a contemporary look, pick two or three main colors in similar tones and mix in lots of white.

Composition

Use an uneven number of strips; depending on the mattress size, three or five look best.

Pattern

Repeat every print several times, sprinkling them throughout so that each one appears in every row.

Prints

To add interest, mix small- and large-scale prints, geometrics and florals, and solids and prints.

04

PERSONAL STYLE

A handbag, a decorative accessory for your living room, a skirt for a little girl—these are projects even a novice sewer will probably feel comfortable attempting. But often people seem much more hesitant to try making an item of clothing that they'll actually wear themselves. I know I felt this way for a long time, until I figured out that sewing clothes wasn't as difficult as I thought. In fact, depending on the pattern, making a dress is often easier than making a handbag!

The clothing projects in this chapter are simple, stylish, practical, and completely achievable even by a novice sewer. I included pieces that are really versatile. Clothing that, depending on the fabric used, could be worn to work, to a party, or just for a casual weekend brunch. The simplicity and classic charm of the Chloe Strapless Dress makes it a great first dress to make. Also, because most people wear some form of knit garment almost every day, I've included some very wearable, easy knit projects. There's a supereasy corsage flower to wear in your hair, on your dress, or to add a bit of sweetness to your bag. And for the stylish men and boys in your life, there's a necktie project that's actually just as cute for a girl.

CAMILLE PLEATED SKIRT

This is a stylish yet comfortable everyday, run-around skirt. It's great for all seasons, depending on your fabric, and looks just as cute whether it's paired with leggings and boots or bare legs and flats. The skirt as designed falls just above the knee, but you can easily lengthen or shorten it to suit your figure or for different occasions. If you've never sewn a zipper into a garment before, fear not. It's really not difficult. Use a ¼" (6mm) seam allowance unless the directions specify otherwise.

FINISHED MEASUREMENTS

SIZE	WAIST	HIPS
2	24½" (62cm)	35½" (90cm)
4	25½" (65cm)	36½" (93cm)
6	26½" (67cm)	37½" (95.5cm)
8	27½" (70cm)	38½" (98cm)
10	28½" (72cm)	39½" (100cm)
12	30" (76cm)	41" (104cm)
14	31½" (80cm)	42½" (108cm)

YARDAGE

1 ¾ yd (1.6m) of 44/45" (112/114cm) cotton print (if you plan to lengthen the skirt, you may need up to 2 yd [1.8m]; see step 1 below)

SUPPLIES

- Camille Skirt pattern
- Your Sewing Box
- 7" (18cm) zipper in a coordinating color
- Seam ripper

STEP 1. *cut out the pieces.*

Using the Camille Skirt pattern, cut out two skirt pieces from your fabric. The pattern calls for the hemline to fall just above the knee and includes ½" (13mm) for the waistband and 1" (2.5cm) for the hem. To lengthen or shorten it, redraw the hemline on both pieces using the existing hemline as a guide. Be sure to keep the A-line angle consistent no matter what the length.

SKIRT LAYOUT

Redraw the hemline up or down to achieve the desired length.

22"

SKIRT   SKIRT

selvage

fold

63"

STEP 2. *sew the darts.*

Transfer the pleat and dart markings from the pattern to the wrong side of the fabric using a pencil. Cut out darts and sew them with right sides together, starting at the wide end and sewing down toward the point. The essential thing is to keep sewing at that same angle right off the fabric. This will give you a smooth dart with no puckering.

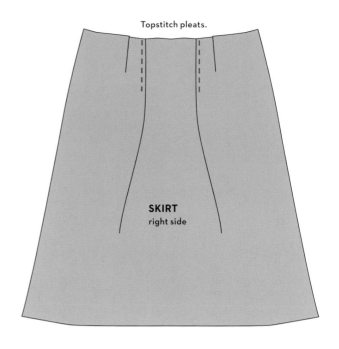
Topstitch pleats.

SKIRT
right side

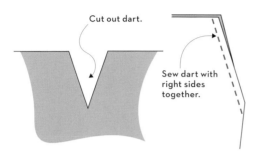

Cut out dart.

Sew dart with right sides together.

STEP 3. *make the pleats.*

Fold the pleats and press. Pin the pleats in place at the waist and 5" (12.5cm) below that. On the right side of the skirt, topstitch each pleat ⅛" (3mm) from the folded edge of the pleat and down 5" (12.5cm). You can sew down the pleats a bit more to make them longer; this will make the top of the skirt narrower. To see if you like this look, pin the pleats down a few more inches (or centimeters) and try on the skirt.

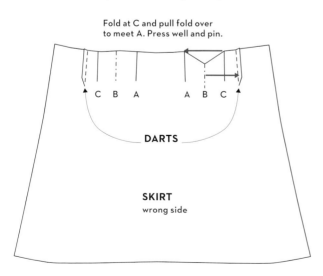

Fold at C and pull fold over to meet A. Press well and pin.

C B A   A B C

DARTS

SKIRT
wrong side

STEP 4. *sew side seams and finish the top.*

With right sides together, pin and sew one side seam. Pin the other side, and sew the first 7½" (19cm) from the top using a basting stitch; this will make it easier to sew in the zipper. Sew the rest of the seam using a regular stitch. Press both seams open. Press the top edge of the skirt under by ¼" (6mm); repeat and topstitch ⅛" (3mm) from the edge.

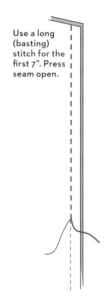

Use a long (basting) stitch for the first 7". Press seam open.

STEP 5. *sew in the zipper.*

Fold and press the top ¹/₂" (13mm) of the zipper toward
the wrong side. Center the closed zipper face down on the
wrong side of the seam, and hand-baste (or pin) it in place,
aligning the folded edge with the top edge of the skirt.
Using a zipper foot, or hand-sewing if you don't have one,
start sewing 2" (5cm) from the top of the zipper. Sew down
one side of the zipper very close to the middle of the zipper.
Turn and sew across the bottom and then back up the other
side, stopping 2" (5cm) before the top. Carefully snip the
basting stitches in the skirt's side seam down the length of
the zipper to open the zipper up. Open the zipper, pulling
the tab down and out of the way. With the zipper open,
qfinish stitching the top 2" (5cm) of each side of the zipper.

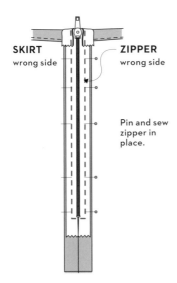

SKIRT
wrong side

ZIPPER
wrong side

Pin and sew
zipper in
place.

STEP 6. *finish the edge.*

Fold the bottom edge of the skirt to the wrong side by ¹/₂"
(13mm) and press. Repeat and topstitch close to the folded
edge.

CHLOE STRAPLESS DRESS

Completely feminine and romantic, this dress with a full skirt, fitted bodice, and optional straps is just fun to wear when you want to feel pretty. Though the bodice is fitted, I added a ruched effect to the back so that it will stay put while allowing you to move and breathe comfortably. Depending on the fabric you choose, this dress silhouette is perfect for a summer picnic, a wedding, or a day at the market. Use a ¼" (6mm) seam allowance unless the directions specify otherwise.

STEP 1. *cut out the pieces.*

Using the Chloe Bodice pattern pieces and the Saturday Gathered Skirt pattern, cut out two skirts (on the fold), one Bodice Front (on the fold), one Bodice Back (on the fold), two Bodice Side Fronts, and two Bodice Side Backs, as shown in the diagram.

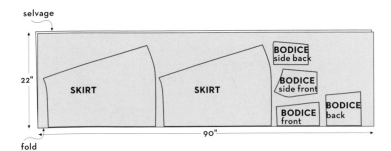

FINISHED MEASUREMENTS

SIZE	BUST	WAIST	HIPS
2	32" (81cm)	24½" (62cm)	35½" (90cm)
4	33" (84cm)	25½" (65cm)	36½" (93cm)
6	34" (86cm)	26½" (67cm)	37½" (95.5cm)
8	35" (89cm)	27½" (70cm)	38½" (98cm)
10	36" (91cm)	28½" (72cm)	39½" (100cm)
12	37½" (95cm)	30" (76cm)	41" (104cm)
14	39" (99cm)	31½" (80cm)	42½" (108cm)

YARDAGE

2½ yd (2.3m) of 44/45" (112/114cm) cotton print for the dress

¼ yd (23cm) of 44/45" (112/114cm) cotton print for the straps (optional)

¼ yd (23cm) of 44/45" coordinating cotton for facing

SUPPLIES

- Chloe Bodice Front, Bodice Back, Bodice Side Front, and Bodice Side Back patterns
- Saturday Gathered Skirt pattern
- Your Sewing Box
- Elastic thread
- All-purpose polyester thread that coordinates with your fabric
- A length of ½" (13mm) elastic the measurement of your waist plus a few inches

STEP 2. *sew the bodice.*

Aligning the side seams and with right sides together, sew the Bodice Front to the Bodice Side Front pieces. With right sides together, sew the Bodice Side Back pieces to the Bodice Side Front pieces. With right sides together, sew the Bodice Back piece to one Bodice Side Back piece.

STEP 3. *make the facing.*

Open the bodice up, and with right sides together, spread it out on top of the facing fabric. Trace the top edge of the bodice onto the facing fabric. Trace the sides of the bodice down 1½" (3.8cm). Draw a parallel line that follows the contours of the top traced line 1½" (3.8cm) below that line onto the facing fabric. Cut out the facing piece. With right sides together, sew the facing to the top of the bodice. If you're going to add straps that tie around the neck, leave a 1" (2.5cm) space for each strap next to the seam that joins the Bodice Side Front to the Bodice Front.

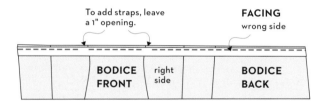

STEP 4. *make the straps (optional).*

If you don't want to add straps, skip to step 5.

Fold both strap pieces in half lengthwise with right sides facing and press. Sew down the long side of the strap, and turn it inside out using a safety pin. If you've never done this before, pin a safety pin to the opening at one end, and then insert the head of the pin into the same opening it's pinned to. Gather the fabric along the pin, and pull it backward until the pin comes out the other side and the strap is turned right side out. Press the straps. Insert 1" (2.5cm) of the straps between the bodice and the facing. Pin and sew in place. Fold the ends of both straps to the inside ¼" (6mm), press, and topstitch ⅛" (3mm) from the end of the strap.

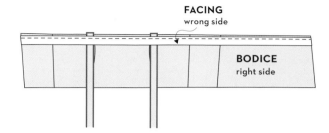

STEP 5. *finish the bodice.*

With right sides together, sew the Bodice Back piece to the Bodice Side Back piece. Fold the facing over the raw edge and press well.

STEP 6. *sew and gather the skirt.*

With right sides together, sew down the sides of the skirt. Stretch the elastic around your waist to a tension that is comfortable and not too tight. Cut the elastic to 1" (2.5cm) longer than that length. Overlap the ends of the elastic by ½" (13mm), and sew them together, backstitching a couple of times to secure. To distribute the elastic evenly around the waist of the skirt, do the following: On the inside of the skirt along the top edge, pin the elastic to the side seam and sew in place using a couple of back-and-forth stitches to tack it to the skirt. Stretch the elastic to the other side seam; pin and tack. Pin and tack the middle front of the elastic to the middle front of the skirt. Repeat on the back of the skirt. Now you can sew the elastic all around the waist of the skirt. As you sew, you'll need to gently stretch the elastic in between the tacking points to the same size as the fabric.

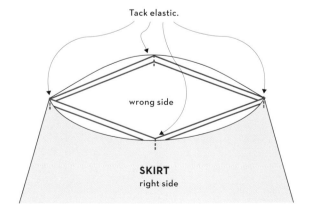

STEP 7. *join the skirt to the bodice.*

With right sides together, place the skirt inside the bodice. Align the bottom edge of the bodice with the top gathered edge of the skirt. The goal now is to stretch the skirt evenly around the bodice the same way you stretched the elastic around the skirt in step 6. You'll see that the back of the bodice is a little bigger than the front. This is because the center back of the bodice will be gathered with elastic thread a little later, so don't let that throw you off.

First pin one side seam of the skirt to one side seam of the bodice. (Remember that the side seams of the bodice are where the Bodice Side Front pieces meet the Bodice Side Back pieces; it's easy to get this wrong if you're not paying close attention.) Sew in place to tack. Stretch the other side seam of the skirt to meet the other side seam of the bodice; pin and tack. Pin and tack the middle of the gathered front skirt edge to the middle of the front bodice edge. Pin and tack the middle of the gathered back skirt edge to the middle of the bodice center back edge. The tacking helps ensure the gathers of the skirt will be evenly distributed.

Now you can sew all around the waist to join the skirt to the bodice. Like sewing the elastic to the skirt, as you sew you'll need to gently stretch the skirt in between the tacking to the same size as the bodice.

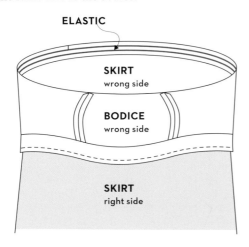

STEP 8. *shirr with elastic thread.*

Review the tips for shirring (page 74), and then wind your bobbin with elastic thread by hand and set your machine at the longest stitch. Starting $\frac{1}{8}$" (3mm) from the top edge of the bodice, on the exterior of the garment, shirr the Bodice Back (but not the Bodice Side Back pieces). Sew lines of elastic stitches $\frac{1}{4}$" (6mm) apart from the top of the Bodice Back to the waistline. Steam the stitches with an iron set to steam in order to gather them. Tie the ends of the elastic threads together in knots.

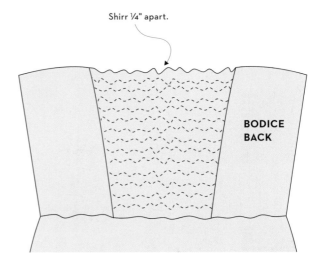

STEP 9. *hem the skirt.*

Fold and press the bottom edge of the skirt to the wrong side by $\frac{1}{2}$" (13mm). Repeat. Topstitch the hem $\frac{3}{8}$" (1cm) from the folded edge.

SATURDAY GATHERED SKIRT

Gathered skirts like this one are classics that can be made trendy, especially in shorter lengths with a ruffle. On this skirt, shirring around the waist and hips forms a comfortable, flattering yoke that moves with you. It can be made in any length and in a variety of fabrics. For summer, sew it in cotton gauze, and wear it with sandals. For winter, the skirt is perfect in a longer length and a dark print. The pattern is actually the skirt portion of the Chloe Strapless Dress (page 122), but you could attach it to any style bodice that has a waistline smaller than the skirt waist. Use a ¼" (6mm) seam allowance unless the directions specify otherwise.

FINISHED MEASUREMENTS

SIZE	WAIST	HIPS
2	24½" (62cm)	35½" (90cm)
4	25½" (65cm)	36½" (93cm)
6	26½" (67cm)	37½" (95.5cm)
8	27½" (70cm)	38½" (98cm)
10	28½" (72cm)	39½" (100cm)
12	30" (76cm)	41" (104cm)
14	31½" (80cm)	42½" (108cm)

YARDAGE

1¾ yd (1.6m) of 44/45" (112/114cm) cotton print fabric for the skirt

1½ yd (1.4m) of 44/45" (112/114cm) contrasting or matching cotton print fabric for the ruffle (optional)

SUPPLIES

• Saturday Gathered Skirt pattern

• Your Sewing Box

• Elastic thread

STEP 1. *cut out the skirt.*

Using the Saturday Gathered Skirt pattern, cut two skirts. The pattern is for a skirt that falls just above the knee (without the ruffle) when worn at the natural waist and includes a 2" (5cm) hem. The ruffle adds about 6" (15cm) to the length. To lengthen or shorten the skirt, measure from the hemline, and draw the length where you'd like, using the pattern as your guide. Keep the angle consistent no matter what the length.

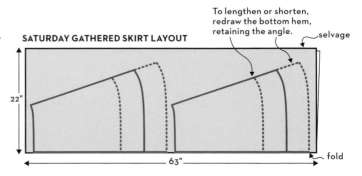

SATURDAY GATHERED SKIRT LAYOUT

To lengthen or shorten, redraw the bottom hem, retaining the angle.

selvage

22"

63"

fold

STEP 2. *sew the side seams.*

With right sides together, align the skirt side seams and sew. Press the seams open. If you're making the ruffle, proceed to step 3. If not, press 1" (2.5cm) of the bottom edge of the skirt to the wrong side; repeat. Pin and topstitch close to the edge, and then go to step 4.

STEP 3. *make the ruffle.*

Measure the front hem of your skirt, and add 5½" (14cm); this will be the width of one half of your ruffle. Cut two ruffles, each 7" (18cm) long by this measurement. With right sides facing, sew the short sides of the ruffles together. Press the seams open. Press the bottom edge of the ruffle under by ¼" (6mm). Press under another ¼" (6mm), and topstitch close to the folded edge. Without locking your stitches (or backstitching), sew the ruffle ⅛" (3mm) from the raw edge using a long basting stitch. Make a second row of basting stitches ⅛" (3mm) from the first one. Pull the top threads of both basted rows at one end to gather the ruffle to the same size as the bottom edge of the skirt, distributing the gathers evenly.

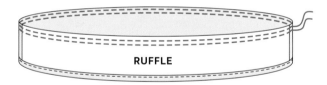

RUFFLE

STEP 4. *attach the ruffle.*

With right sides together and side seams aligned, pin the gathered edge of the ruffle to the bottom edge of the skirt. Sew the ruffle and skirt together.

STEP 5. *shirr the waist with elastic thread.*

Press the top of the skirt under by ¾" (2cm). Review the tips for shirring (page 74), wind your bobbin with elastic thread by hand, and set your machine at the longest stitch. Starting at a side seam, topstitch on the right side (outside) of the skirt ¼" (6mm) from the top folded edge, and continue all around. When you reach the starting point, dip down diagonally by ¼" (6mm), and continue sewing ¼" (6mm) down from the first row of stitches all around. Repeat until you've completed six rows of elastic stitches. You can sew a few more rows if you'd like more of a yoke effect. Steam the stitching using an iron set to steam. It should gather up quite a bit.

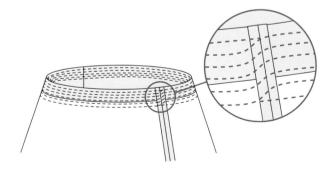

CORSAGE
FLOWERS

CORSAGE FLOWERS

There are many ways to make fabric flowers, but this is one of my favorites. The final effect is similar to an old-fashioned millinery flower, the kind that ladies once wore on their hats and dresses, but this is much easier to make. For a modern take on vintage charm, pin it to your handbag, stitch it to the strap or waistline of a dress, or sew it to a bobby pin, barrette, or elastic band and wear it in your hair. Though these corsages are sweet made with prints, for a more realistic-looking flower, choose solid-color fabrics that are, the same color on both sides. Gauze works well because it's lightweight and easy to sew through several layers. Linen and silk work beautifully, as well. The trick to making these flowers, one that my grandmother used for various delicate crafts, is to use heavy spray starch before cutting the fabric into flowery shapes. The starch makes it stiff, gives it body, and prevents fraying.

FINISHED MEASUREMENTS

Large flower: 6½" (16.5cm) wide

Medium flower: 4½" (11.5cm) wide

YARDAGE

Bits of gauze, linen, dupioni silk, voile, organdy, or other light-weight fabric

Green fabric scraps for leaves (optional)

SUPPLIES

- Your Sewing Box

- Heavy spray starch (available in grocery stores)

- Coordinating upholstery/carpet thread

- One faux pearl or bead with a hole for threading (broken costume jewelry is great to use) for each flower

STEP 1. *cut out the circles.*

For the medium flower, cut two circles 4$\frac{1}{2}$" in diameter, two circles 3$\frac{1}{2}$" in diameter, two circles 2$\frac{1}{2}$" in diameter, and two circles 1$\frac{1}{2}$" in diameter. For the large flower, cut two more circles 5$\frac{1}{2}$" in diameter.

STEP 2. *stiffen the fabric.*

Lightly spray each fabric circle with spray starch. Be sure to shake the spray starch well or it will not spray correctly and the fabric will get too wet. Set your iron to high for 100 percent cotton fabric and lower as appropriate for silks and synthetics. Iron each circle until it is completely dry and somewhat stiff. Repeat spray starch and ironing once more. The fabric should have the stiffness of a piece of paper at this point.

STEP 3. *cut the flower shapes.*

Cut a wavy shape around the edge of one of the largest circles. Cut a wavy edge around another of the largest circles, but cut it so that it is a little smaller than the first. Cut a wavy edge around all the circles in this way, slightly graduating down in the size of each successive flower layer.

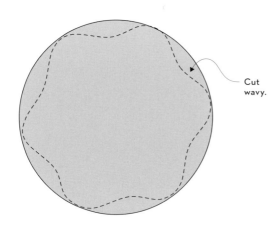

Cut wavy.

STEP 4. *sew and gather the layers.*

Arrange the layers in order of size with the smallest one on top. Rotate all the flower shapes to get a natural look, and pin them together. Thread a needle with strong upholstery or carpet thread, and tie both thread ends together into a single knot. Stitch a circle $\frac{3}{4}$" (2cm) in diameter in the center of the flower through all layers, ending with the needle coming through the back of the flower. Pull the thread to gather. As you gather, gently push the center of the pucker to the back of the flower with your pinky or a pencil. Continue to pull and gather as much as you can without breaking the thread or pulling the knotted end through.

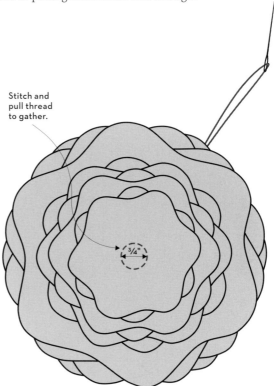

Stitch and pull thread to gather.

$\frac{3}{4}$"

STEP 5. *secure the thread.*

Make a couple of small stitches on the center back of the flower. Pass the needle under these stitches a couple of times, and make a knot to secure. Thread and knot the needle as before, and sew from the center back of the flower through to the center front, through each bead and back through the center to the back of the flower. Repeat and secure with a couple stitches and a knot.

STEP 6. *add leaves (optional).*

To add leaves, stiffen fabric with heavy starch and iron. Cut desired leaf shapes. Fold each leaf in half and press. Sew to the back of the flower.

I LOVE YOU NECKTIE

This is a really fun thing to make for one (or more) of the men, boys, or even girls in your life. I once thought there was a mystique to creating a great tie, but as it turns out, they are easy to make. And, while sewing something that a man will actually like isn't usually easy, this project is a pretty safe bet. The fabric possibilities are endless, including today's gorgeous cottons or traditional silks. This project entails mostly hand stitching, but don't worry—it's just enough handwork to be relaxing and not annoying. Use a 1/4" (6mm) seam allowance unless the directions specify otherwise.

FINISHED MEASUREMENTS
54½" long x 3½" wide (138cm x 9cm)

YARDAGE
For the tie: 1 yd (91cm) of 44/45" (112/114cm) cotton print

For the lining: 9" x 16" (23cm x 40.5cm) piece of print or solid cotton

1 yd (91cm) of 20" (51cm) light-weight sew-in interfacing

SUPPLIES
- Tie A, B, and C patterns
- Your Sewing Box

STEP 1. *cut out the pieces.*

Place the fabric right side down on a table, and fold up the lower left corner just enough to fit the Tie B pattern piece when placed on the fold. Pin the pattern on the fold, and cut out B. Fold the same corner up enough to fit the Tie C pattern, pin on the fold, and cut. Repeat for Tie A pattern.

CUTTING LAYOUT FOR TIE

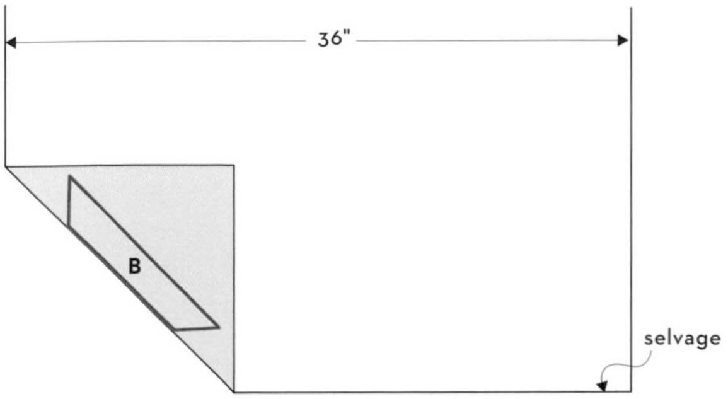

36"

B

selvage

STEP 2. *cut off the triangles.*

Open up the tie pieces, and place the patterns on top. Using a ruler and pencil, extend the dotted diagonal lines on the fabric exactly as shown. Trim off the triangles on one side only.

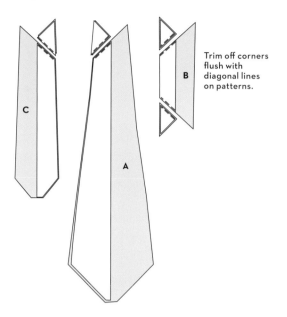

Trim off corners flush with diagonal lines on patterns.

STEP 3. *sew the tie.*

With right sides together, pin and sew A to B at a 90-degree angle, and then do the same with C to B. Press the seams open.

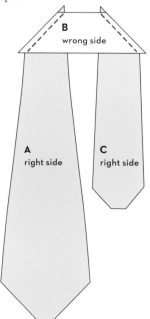

STEP 4. *make the points.*

On both ends of the tie, press the tip under by ³⁄₈" (1cm). Fold the diagonal edges under to form a neat point on both ends and press. On the lining pieces, press the tips under by ¹⁄₂" (13mm), and then form the points and press.

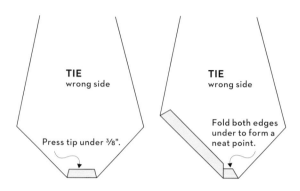

STEP 5. *sew the sides together.*

With right sides together, place the lining point ¹⁄₈" (3mm) above the tie point, and sew the sides of the lining and tie together using a ³⁄₈" (1cm) seam. Turn right side out and press. Whipstitch the diagonal edges of the lining to the tie on both ends, sewing only through the lining and the folded edges of the tie so that the stitches don't show on the front.

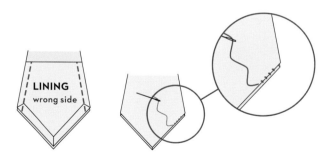

STEP 6. *shape the tie.*

Press the long edges under by ³⁄₈" (1cm). Fold the tie in half crosswise, and insert a pin at the fold to mark the middle of the tie. On the wide end, measure from the point up both angled sides 2³⁄₄" (7cm). Beginning at this point, press the side edges in, overlapping them, until you reach the midpoint pin, pinning the layers together as you go. The tie should measure about 1¹⁄₂" (3.8cm) at the midpoint. On the narrow end, measure up only 1¼" (3cm), and repeat the folding and pinning process to the midpoint from the other direction.

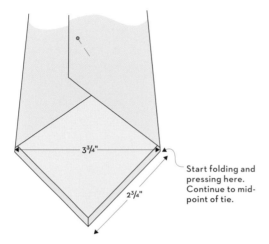

3¾"

2¾"

Start folding and pressing here. Continue to midpoint of tie.

STEP 7. *cut out the interfacing.*

Place the tie on top of the interfacing, and trace from the midpoint around the narrow end. Add ⅛" (3mm) to the midpoint end, and cut out the interfacing. Trace around the wide end, again adding ⅛" (3mm) at the midpoint, and cut it out. Trim the interfacing, if necessary, so that it fits inside the tie without interfering with the shape.

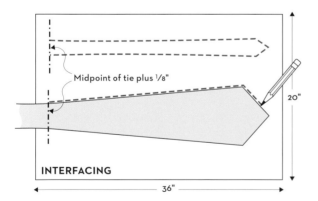

Midpoint of tie plus ⅛"

20"

INTERFACING

36"

STEP 8. *insert the interfacing.*

Remove the pins in the tie, and insert the interfacings into the lining pockets. Tack the interfacing to the lining with a few loose hand stitches. Overlap the interfacing pieces in the middle, and tack them together with a hand stitch loosely.

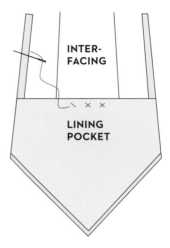

INTER-FACING

LINING POCKET

STEP 9. *fold the tie back into its final shape.*

Pin the overlapped edges of the tie together again, and slip-stitch them loosely, making the stitches as invisible as you can by sewing them slightly under the edge of the overlapping top fold through the bottom fold, making sure not to go through or catch the front of the tie in your stitches.

Knits

NOT SO SCARY AFTER ALL

Knits—called such because the threads used to create the fabric are literally knitted into tiny little knots as opposed to being woven—are wonderfully comfortable to wear, as they stretch and move with you. They also tend to be flattering and are relatively inexpensive, as fabrics go. Although we all wear some variety of knit garment almost every day (T-shirts, underwear, sportswear, casual wear, etc.), many people are reluctant to sew with knits unless they have a serger, which is a nifty but pricey sewing machine that finishes the raw edge of a garment by neatly encasing it in stitches that allow the fabric to stretch and move. Check out the seams inside almost any factory-made garment in your closet, and you'll see what I mean. While a serger is nice to have, it isn't really necessary. A simple zigzag stitch works just fine for the home sewer. Why the zigzag? Because stretchy fabric needs a stitch that will stretch with it or else the stitches will break when the fabric is stretched.

To be honest, knits can be a bit more unpredictable than woven fabrics in terms of how they interact with your sewing machine. Though all the knit projects in this book were sewn on my basic, inexpensive sewing machine, I can't guarantee the same results with your machine. The biggest potential problem comes from the fabric being flattened and stretched out too much under the pressure of the presser foot. But you may be able to adjust this. Read the guide that came with your machine, and make the necessary adjustments; then practice so that you know exactly what to expect.

For the knit projects in this book, I recommend using a single-knit fabric, such as jersey, with two-way stretch. *Two-way stretch* means the fabric stretches both vertically and horizontally. (Confusingly, this is also sometimes referred to as *four-way stretch*.) Two-way-stretch knit will usually stretch more in one direction than the other. Always cut your fabric so that it stretches the most horizontally around your body where you need more stretch, rather than vertically.

Before you jump in with both feet, you might want to practice sewing pieces of an old T-shirt. Adjust your machine as indicated by the manufacturer, and zigzag a couple of layers together. Make any other adjustments needed until you're satisfied with the stitching. Once you've had some practice, go ahead and buy your beautiful knit fabric. Sewing with knits opens up a world of new options for making really practical and flattering clothing that you'll wear every day, so I hope you'll give it a try.

Important Tips for Sewing Knits

• Follow your sewing machine's instructions regarding tension and other settings.

• Use a ballpoint needle in the correct size for best results.

• Place the pattern pieces on the knit fabric in the same direction.

• Do not pull or stretch the knit fabric too much as you sew.

• Use all-purpose polyester thread.

• To prevent inadvertent stretching, don't let your fabric hang down off your sewing surface as you sew.

• Use a narrow zigzag stitch for all sewing—except for shirring with elastic thread, when you should use a straight stitch.

FAST AND EASY KNIT PROJECT IDEAS

Superquick Knit Cowl

These are fun to make in all different colors for gifts. They give just enough warmth to the neck on a chilly day but can be worn inside without making the wearer too hot.

Neatly and precisely cut cotton knit fabric with two-way stretch to 64" x 28" (163cm x 71cm) so that the 64" (163cm) length has the most stretch. Cut very carefully; since you won't be finishing the raw edges, they have to look really neat for this to work. Sew the two short ends together. To wear the cowl, loop it twice around your neck.

Two-Color Scarf

From stretchy light-weight knit fabric in two different colors, cut two rectangles, each 63" long x 12" wide (160cm x 30.5cm) or any desired width—narrow scarves are very popular these days. Zigzag the two pieces together along the edges, leaving a 5" (12.5cm) opening for turning. Turn right side out, and finish the opening with a whipstitch. Leave plain or decorate the scarf with felt or wool appliqués or flowers.

LA DOLCE VITA BLOUSE

The peasant blouse, long a part of the folk dress of many cultures from Eastern Europe to Mexico, saw a resurgence in popularity in the 1940s that continues today. This updated version in cotton knit features shirring at the neck, sleeves (optional), and waist, giving it a more fitted look, and it can be worn on or off the shoulder. Make it plain or use contrasting brightly colored top threads, or try a pretty printed knit. Use a ¼" (6mm) seam allowance unless the directions specify otherwise.

FINISHED MEASUREMENTS

SIZE	BUST
S	32" to 34" (81cm–86cm)
M	35" to 36" (89cm–91cm)
L	37" to 39" (94cm–99cm)

YARDAGE

1¾ yd (91cm) of 60" (152.5cm) or wider two- or four-way stretch jersey knit, cotton or cotton-blend

SUPPLIES

• La Dolce Vita Blouse pattern

• Your Sewing Box

• Elastic thread

• Ballpoint sewing-machine needle

• All-purpose polyester thread that coordinates with your fabric

---

STEP 1. *cut out the pieces.*

First review the tips on page 136 for working with knits. Pin the La Dolce Vita Blouse pattern to the fabric on the fold, and cut two.

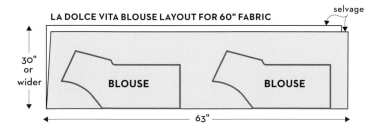

LA DOLCE VITA BLOUSE LAYOUT FOR 60" FABRIC

selvage

30" or wider

BLOUSE   BLOUSE

63"

STEP 2. *join the front and back.*

With right sides facing, sew the front and back pieces together at the shoulder and side seams, using a narrow zigzag stitch.

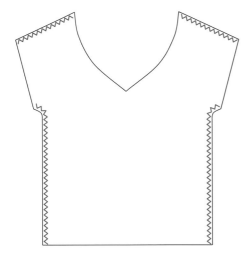

STEP 3. *finish the edges.*

Make a ³/₄" (2cm) vertical slit at the center of the front and back neckline.

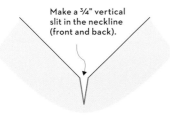

Make a ¾" vertical slit in the neckline (front and back).

Fold the top edge of the neck opening to the inside by a little more than ³/₄" (2cm) and pin. Fold the bottom edge to the inside by 1¼" (3cm) and pin. For a plain sleeve, fold the raw edge under by ¹/₄" (6mm), and topstitch over the raw edge using a narrow zigzag stitch. See step 4 for making a shirred sleeve.

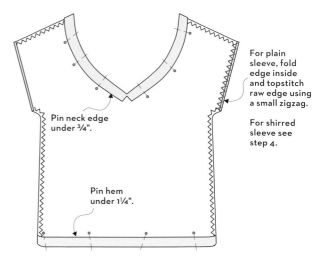

For plain sleeve, fold edge inside and topstitch raw edge using a small zigzag.

For shirred sleeve see step 4.

Pin neck edge under ¾".

Pin hem under 1¼".

STEP 4. *shirr the neckline, waist, and sleeves.*

Review the tips for shirring on page 74, and then wind your bobbin with elastic thread by hand, and set your machine at the longest stitch. To shirr the neckline, use a straight stitch and start at the shoulder seam on the garment exterior, and sew around the neckline ¹/₄" (6mm) from the folded edge. Sew a second row ¹/₄" (6mm) from the first row. To shirr the sleeves, fold the sleeve edge under by ¹/₄" (6mm) and pin. Starting at the underarm seam, sew ¹/₈" (3mm) from the folded edge. As you approach the starting point, dip down ¹/₄" (6mm), and make a second row of shirring. (See step 5 diagram on page 128.) To shirr the waist, starting at a side seam, sew all around the waist ¹/₄" (6mm) from the folded edge, dipping down diagonally by ¹/₄" (6mm) as you reach the starting point and continuing to sew. Make a total of ten rows of shirring at the waist.

When you're done, lightly steam the elastic stitching with an iron set to steam. It should gather up quite a bit.

GO-TO TOP
OR DRESS

GO-TO TOP OR DRESS

This dress is really comfortable, flattering, versatile, and easy to make. A shirred waist gives it a feminine feel, but the overall look is chic. The modern shape works really well in cotton or cotton-blend knit jersey. Make a casual long top to wear with a chunky leather belt and jeans, a charcoal gray dress for the office, or a little black date dress that's sexy and comfy. This garment should be made with a light-weight knit with two-way stretch. Make the sleeve opening a little bigger for a more kimonolike sleeve or smaller for a drapey cap sleeve. Or shirr the sleeve at the shoulder to get a kind of Greek-goddess look. The pattern is for a dress that falls above the knee but can also be made as a top by cutting the skirt portion to a shorter length. Use a ¼" (6mm) seam allowance unless the directions specify otherwise.

FINISHED MEASUREMENTS

SIZE	BUST	WAIST
S	32" to 33" (81cm–84cm)	24½" to 25½" (62cm–65cm)
M	34" to 35" (86cm–89cm)	26½" to 27½" (67cm–70cm)
L	36" to 38" (91cm–96.5cm)	28½" to 30" (72cm–76cm)
XL	39" (99cm)	31" to 32" (79cm–80cm)

YARDAGE

2½ yd (2.3m) of 58" (147cm) or wider light-weight cotton or cotton-blend two-tor four-way stretch jersey knit

SUPPLIES

- Go-to Top and Bottom patterns
- Your Sewing Box
- Ballpoint sewing-machine needle
- All-purpose polyester thread that coordinates with your fabric
- Elastic thread
- Quilter's chalk (optional)

STEP 1. *cut out the pieces.*

First review the tips on page 136 for working with knits. Using the Go-to Top and Bottom patterns, place the pieces on the fold as shown in the diagram, and cut them out. Make sure to cut the fabric so that it stretches the most horizontally across and around the body. If you don't, your finished garment won't fit around your curves.

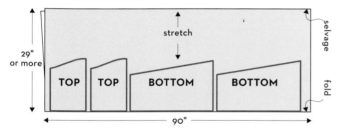

GO-TO DRESS LAYOUT

STEP 2. *sew the top pieces together.*

With right sides together, pin the longest edges of the Top pieces together. Sew in 6" (15cm) from both ends, or sew in 6" (15cm) using a narrow zigzag stitch, leaving the middle section open. (For a lower, more revealing neckline, you can sew in 6"(15cm) on one side and 4" (10cm) on the other. In this case, the 6" (15cm) side would be the back of the dress).

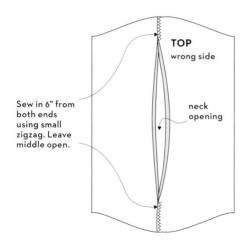

STEP 3. *sew the skirt pieces to the top.*

With right sides together, start in the middle of the seam (with knits it's often better to start in the middle and sew outward to the side, go back to the middle, and repeat in the other direction), and sew the Bottom pieces to the Top using a narrow zigzag stitch. As you sew, hold the ends of the fabric together, and stretch just barely enough to make sure the seams match up.

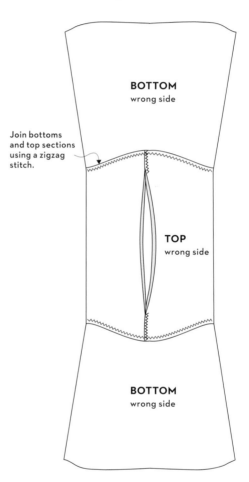

STEP 4. *sew the side seams.*

With right sides together, match up the waist seams. Starting 4½" (11.5cm) above the waist seam for a cap sleeve or 2" (5cm) above the waist seam for a kimonolike sleeve, sew down the length of the side seams using a narrow zigzag stitch.

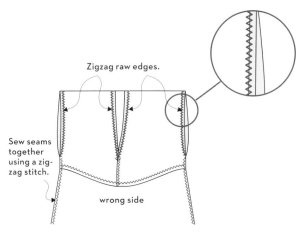

Zigzag raw edges.

Sew seams together using a zig-zag stitch.

wrong side

STEP 5. *finish the neck, sleeves, and hem.*

Fold the raw edges of the neck opening to the inside by ¼" (6mm). Line up the folded raw edge with the middle of the presser foot, and topstitch using a narrow zigzag, making sure you are covering the raw edge with the zigzag (refer to previous diagram). Finish the sleeve edges in the same manner. Before you hem the bottom edge, on both side seams simply trim the bottom of the dress so that it forms a smooth curve, instead of a point, at the seam. You won't be able to hem it properly unless you do this. Fold the bottom hem to the inside by ½" (13mm) and pin. As you did with the sleeves and neck, line up the middle of the presser foot with the raw edge of the folded-over fabric, and zigzag to cover the raw edge.

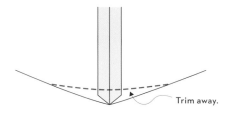

Trim away.

STEP 6. *shirr the waist.*

Review the tips for shirring (page 74), and then wind your bobbin with elastic thread by hand, and set your machine at the longest stitch. Starting at a side seam on the exterior of garment and using a straight stitch, backstitch a couple of times, and then sew very close to the waist seam all the way around, stretching the seam out behind the presser foot as you sew just enough to make sure the fabric doesn't bunch up. When you reach the beginning, dip down diagonally by ¼" (6mm) and continue sewing, making three rows of shirring altogether (see step 5 diagram on page 128). Backstitch a couple of times at the end. Try the garment on to decide if you want to add a few more lines of shirring. The more you add, the more defined the waist will be.

If you'd like, shirr the shoulders, as well. Use quilter's chalk to mark the shoulder fold, and stitch on this line. You can add one more shirring stitch line ¼" (6mm) from the first. When you're done shirring, steam the shirred stitches lightly with an iron set to steam. It should gather up quite a bit.

You can make a matching belt for this project from leftover fabric. Cut a long rectangle of fabric to the desired length plus 1" (2.5cm) and twice the desired width plus ¹/₂" (13mm). With right sides together, fold in half widthwise and stitch the long edge using a zigzag stitch. Turn right side out. Fold the raw edges of the opening to the inside by ¹/₂"(13mm) and topstitch closed using a straight stitch.

EVERYDAY KNIT TUNIC

This tunic is wonderfully flattering, comfortable, and versatile. The focus is on your shoulders and neck, and it's looser at the waist, which most women appreciate. This tunic is supereasy, as well, so you can make a few in no time. Use a ¼" (6mm) seam allowance unless the directions specify otherwise.

STEP 1. *cut out the pattern pieces.*

First review the tips on page 136 for working with knits. Place the Everyday Knit Tunic pattern on the fabric as shown in the diagram, and cut out two.

TUNIC LAYOUT

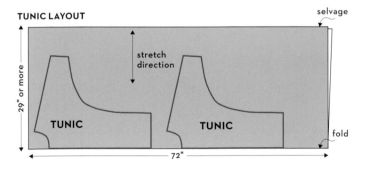

FINISHED MEASUREMENTS

SIZE	BUST
S	32" to 33" (81cm–84cm)
M	34" to 35" (86cm–89cm)
L	36" to 38" (91cm–96.5cm)
XL	39" (99cm)

YARDAGE

2 yd (1.8m) of 58" (147cm) or wider lightweight cotton or cotton-blend two- or four-way stretch jersey knit

SUPPLIES

- Everyday Knit Tunic pattern
- Your Sewing Box
- Ballpoint sewing-machine needle
- All-purpose polyester thread that coordinates with your fabric

STEP 2. *sew the pieces together.*

With right sides together, sew the shoulders from the neckline to the end of the sleeve. Starting from under the sleeve, sew down both sides of the tunic. Then, on both sleeves, sew from under the sleeve to the sleeve opening.

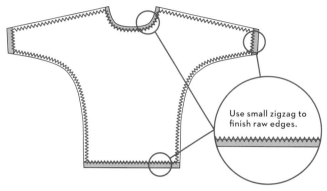

Use small zigzag to finish raw edges.

STEP 3. *finish the raw edges.*

Starting at the shoulder seam, fold the raw edge of the neckline to the inside by $1/4$" (6mm), and line up the raw edge with the center of your presser foot. Sew all around using a small zigzag stitch to cover the raw edge. Keep folding the raw edge to the inside by $1/4$" (6mm) as you sew, and take your time so that you get a nice consistent $1/4$" (6mm) seam. Using the same approach, fold and sew the raw edges of the sleeve to the inside by $1/2$" (13mm). Finish the bottom hem in the same way.

Fabric Resources

Many of the fabrics used in this book were designed by me and other wonderful designers, and manufactured and distributed by Free Spirit. To find a list of shops that carry these fabrics near you, go to www.freespiritfabric.com.

Here are some other great resources:

www.fatquartershop.com
866-826-2069

www.hancocks-paducah.com
800-845-8723

www.sewmamasew.com
503-380-3584

www.equilter.com
877-322-7423

www.quilthome.com
877-684-9001

www.fabric.com
888-455-2940

www.mariemadelinestudio.com
417-775-2181

www.thequiltedcastle.com

www.allegrofabrics.com

www.etsy.com

www.ebay.com

Acknowledgments

Thank you to my children, who are the most important part of my life, the best thing I've ever done, and who make my life worth living every day. Thank you Max, for your patience, helpfulness, and thoughtfulness during the writing of this book. You really, really helped us all to get through this hectic time. I am so proud of you and love you so very much. Thank you to Harry for making me laugh and for engaging me in challenging political and philosophical discussions when I probably should have been working. You always make me think, kid, and that makes me proud. I love you, Harry. Thank you to Ava for so often inspiring my creativity with your amazing sense of design and your creativity, which contributed so much to this book. Most of all, thank you for your sweet and generous spirit. I love you, my sweet, sweet girl.

Thank you to my father, Tom Whelan, for always loving and supporting me.

Thank you to my incredibly talented friend Yvonne Eijkenduijn of Yvestown, for helping me make this book beautiful with your pitch-perfect eye for styling and photography, for the use of your gorgeous home, and for making work fun.

Thank you to the amazing Matthew Mead, for your absolutely gorgeous photography.

Thank you to my uncle, Barry Becker, for helping me with the illustrations and for making this a family affair.

Thank you to the lovely Colleen Mohyde, for helping to make this project happen.

Thank you to my grandmother, Helen Whelan, for giving me my first giant box of quilting fabric and for teaching me to knit, both of which helped open up the world of crafting and creativity to me.

Thank you to my editor, Betty Wong, whose sure, calm, and steady demeanor during this process helped me to keep my neurosis and slight tendency to panic to a minimum.

Thank you to all the wonderful women who helped to test these projects. Thanks especially to the lovely women at Marie Madeline studio: Kristie Long, Apphia Long, Achaia Long, Abigail Long, Abiah Long.

Thank you to my best friends, Elena Lipkins and Sonia Montalbano, for listening to me rant and rave about silly things and for still loving me after all these years.

Thank you to Silva, for all the good luck you bring my way.

Thank you to AP, who brings so much beauty and love to the world through her work, for her insight and humor and for literally being one of the most delightful and real people one could ever wish to have a conversation with.

About the Author

Tanya Whelan is a lifestyle designer of fabrics, homewares, and sewing patterns. Her fabrics are produced and distributed by Free Spirit Fabrics, a subsidiary of Coats and Clark. Her fabrics and sewing patterns are sold under her name worldwide through independent fabric shops and major retailers. Her homewares collections are distributed throughout the U.S. and Canada. She currently lives in Belgium with her husband and children. Visit her at www.grandrevivaldesign.typepad.com.

A
advice, 13
allowance, seam, 15
Amelie bag, 22–25
  apple pie ottoman, 90–92
apron, 102–105

B
baby blocks, soft, 67–69
baby duvet, 62–66
balls, patchwork, 54–57
basting, 12, 14
big easy sling bag, 26–29
blocks, baby, soft, 67–69
blouse(s)
  La Dolce Vita, 137
  shirred, 76–79, 80–83
box
  fabric, 98–101
  sewing, 17

C
Camille pleated skirt, 118–121
checkers, travel, 70–73
children, sewing for, 42–87
Chloe strapless dress, 122–125
city tote, 34–36
clipping curves, 14
clutch, pleated, 37–41
color(s)
  quilt, 115
  two, in scarf, 137
composition, quilt, 115
cone and stacking rings, 44–50
corners, trimming of, 15
corsage flowers, 129–131
cowl, knit, 137
curves, clipping of, 14
cutting, on fold, 14

D
dart, 14
design-as-you-go quilt, 110–115
design guidelines, quilt, 115
Dorothy apron, 102–105
dress
  go-to, 141–145
  strapless, 122–125
  summer, 75
duvet, baby, 62–66

E
easy knit project ideas, 137
easy reversible fabric box or tote, 98–101
easy shirring projects, 75
easy sling bag, 26–29
edges, raw, 14
elastic thread, 74–75
embroidered felt purse, 51–53
everyday knit tunic, 146–148

F
fabric(s)
  principles concerning, 12, 13
  understanding and using, 18–19
fabric box or tote, 98–101
fabric resources, 149
fabric shade, 106–109
fast knit project ideas, 137
fast shirring projects, 75
felt purse, embroidered, 51–53
flattering refit, 75
flowers, corsage, 129–131
fold, cutting on, 14
fussing, 13

G
gathered skirt, 126–128
gathering, 14
giant patchwork ball, 55–56
good sewing principles, 12–13
go-to top or dress, 141–145

H
handmade handbags, 20–41
home style, 88–115
hook-and-loop tape, 14

I
I love you necktie, 132–135
interfacing, 14

J
Juliette shirred blouse, 80–83

K
knits, 19, 136–137
knit tunic, 146–148

L
La Dolce Vita blouse, 138–140
Lila shirred blouse, 76–79
little ones, sewing for, 42–87
locking seams, 12
love, of sewing, 9

M
machine, sewing, children and, 53
made by me! embroidered felt purse, 51–53
materials, 16–19
modern shirring, 74–75

N
necktie, 132–135

O
ottoman, 90–92

P
patchwork balls, 54–57
pattern, print, in quilt, 115
patterns, 17
personal style, 116–148
pieced pincushion, 95
pillowcase sundress, 75
pincushions, 93–97
pinning right way, 12
playing around, 12
pleat, 14
pleated clutch, 37–41
pleated skirt, 118–121
posy pincushion, 96–97
preparing, of fabrics, 12
pressing, 12
pretty pincushions, 93–97
pretty pleated clutch, 37–41
principles, sewing, 12–13
prints, quilt, 115
purse, embroidered felt, 51–53

Q
quilt, design-as-you-go, 110–115

R
raw edges, 14
reading first, sewing second, 12
refit, flattering, 75
resources, fabric, 149
reuse, repurpose, and refashion, 13

reversible fabric box or tote, 98–101
right side, 14
right way, of pinning, 12
rings, stacking, 44–50
ruffle-mania skirt, 58–61
rules, about fabrics, 13

S
safety, child, 53, 109
Saturday gathered skirt, 126–128
scarf, two-color, 137
seam allowance, 15
seams, locking of, 12
sewing
  love of, 9
  as term, 15
sewing box, 17
sewing machine, children and, 53
sewing principles, 12–13
sewing terms, 14–15
shade, fabric, 106–109
shirred blouses, 76–79, 80–83
shirring, modern, 74–75
side
  right, 14
  wrong, 15
skirt
  gathered, 126–128
  pleated, 118–121
  ruffle-mania, 58–61
  tiered, 84–87
sling bag, 26–29
small patchwork balls, 57
soft baby blocks, 67–69
soft fabric shade, 106–109
stacking rings, 44–50
stitches, types of, 15
stitching, as term, 15
stitching in the ditch, 15
strapless dress, 122–125
style
  home, 88–115
  personal, 116–148
sundress, pillowcase, 75
superquick knit cowl, 137
sweet pea baby duvet, 62–66

T
tape, hook-and-loop, 14
tee, terrific, 75
templates, 17
terms, 14–15
terrific tee, 75
thread, elastic, 74–75
tiered skirt, 84–87
tools, 17
top, go-to, 141–145
topstitch, 15
tote
  city, 34–36
  fabric, reversible, 98–101
travel checkers, 70–73
trimming corners, 15
tunic, knit, 146–148
two-color scarf, 137
two pretty pincushions, 93–97

W
whipstitch, 15
wrong side, 15

Y
your sewing box, 17

Z
Zoe bag, 30–33